The Raisin

Rivers of Michigan Series

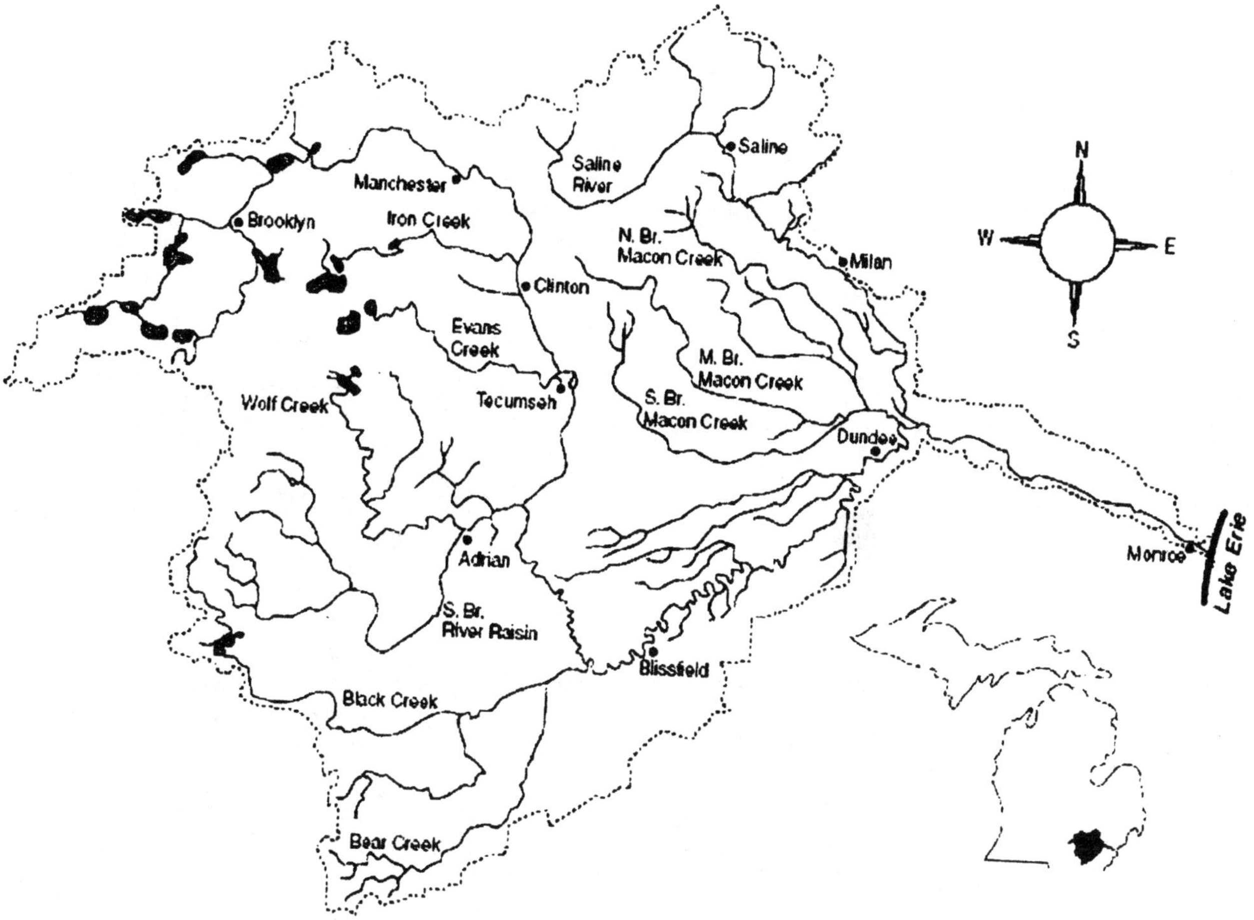

By Kit Lane

Pavilion Press
P.O. Box 250
Douglas, Michigan 49406

Copyright 2009

by Pavilion Press

All Rights Reserved

International Standard Book Number
978-1-877703-04-1

Front Cover: *(Top) Scene on the River Raisin, a group of young boys paddling canoes, on the river near Adrian on a postcard mailed in June, 1912.*

(Bottom) The Government Canal at Monroe about 1910. The Monroe Yacht Club building is at right. The old lighthouse is visible in the distance at left.

Back Cover: *The Monroe lighthouse and keeper's home on the north pier about 1912.*

Table of Contents

The River	4
Natives and Early Visitors	13
Early Settlers	18
War of 1812	23
Floods and Bridges	33
Dams and Power Production	37
Ecological Future	42
From Beginning to End	47
Sources:	
The Goose Creek Connection	51
Main Stream to Brooklyn	57
Brooklyn to Manchester	61
Manchester to Tecumseh	65
Tecumseh to Blissfield	69
Blissfield to Dundee	77
Dundee to Lake Erie	83
Bibliography	101
Index	105

Photo Credits and Acknowledgments

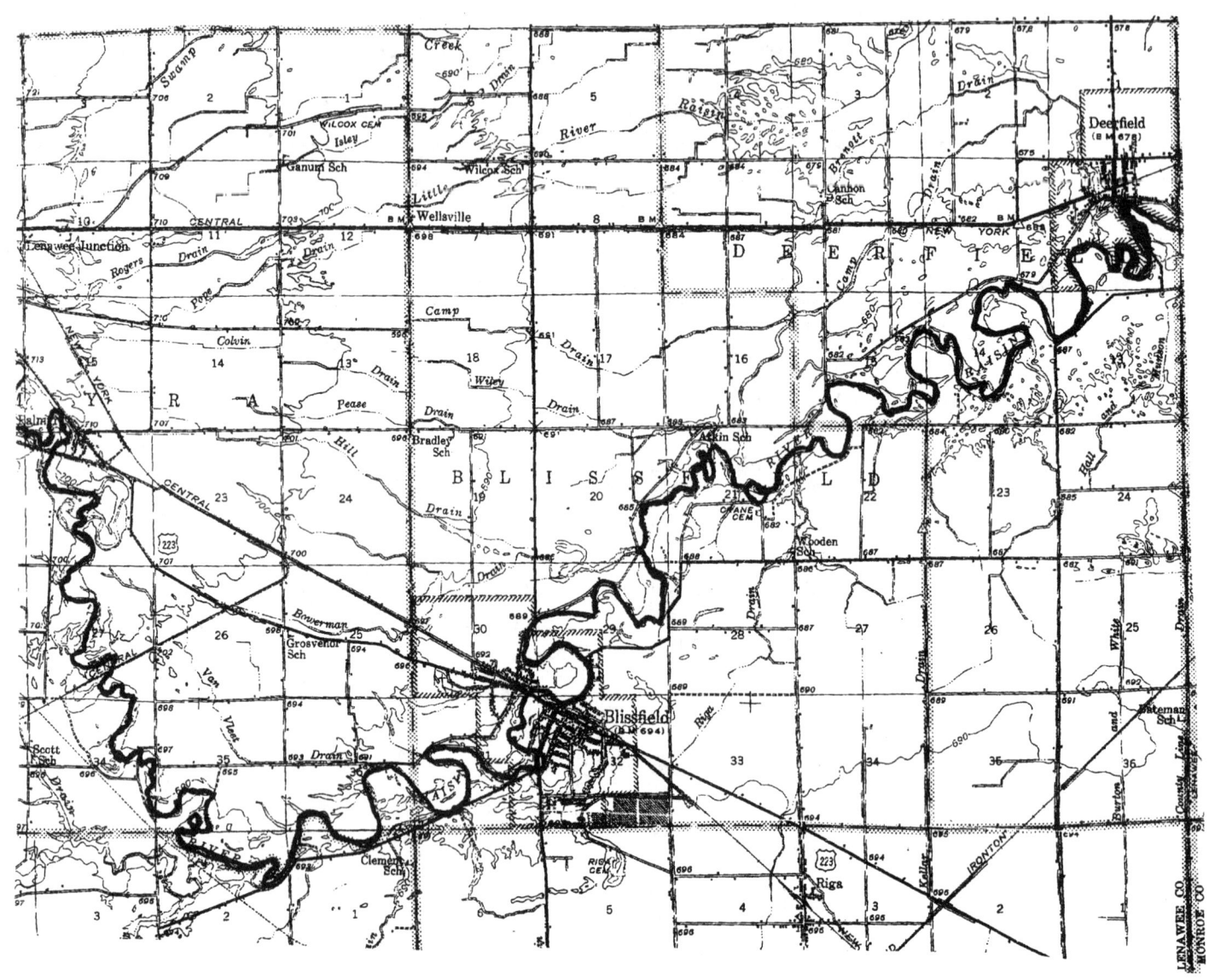

A 1929 survey map showing the river from Palmyra to Deerfield. Legend has it that "Ripley's Believe it or Not!" a syndicated newspaper cartoon which began in 1918, once featured the River Raisin as "the most crooked river in the world," but a copy of the column, or anyone who had actually seen it, could not be located.

The River

> The Raisin river heads in Wheatland township, Hillsdale county, and empties into Lake Erie, two and a half miles below Monroe, after passing, in an extremely winding course, through Jackson, Washtenaw, Lenawee, and Monroe counties. It is the most serpentine stream of the peninsula. Its course is first north-easterly, then south, then north-easterly, and south-easterly. In a direct line from its head to its mouth, it is 60 miles; but by its meanderings, it is not less than 130 miles. It is one of the most important streams in Michigan; affording as much hydraulic power as any other; having high and beautiful banks, and an extremely rapid current; the bottom being a limestone rock, which produces a good quality of building material, is extensively quarried for the purpose. The water power is improved to a considerable extent, and has been the means of building up respectable villages at Manchester, Clinton, Tecumseh, Adrian, Palmyra, Blissfield, Petersburgh, Dundee and Monroe. Its name is derived from the dense clusters of grape vines which formerly lined both banks. [1]

In the quotation above, from John T. Blois in his 1838 *Gazetteer of Michigan* it was the meandering nature of the watercourse which was the outstanding characteristic of the River Raisin.

Blois wasn't the only one impressed by the river's meandering watershed. *Ripley's Believe It or Not!* syndicated feature, it is said, recognized it as the "most crooked river in the world."

Watershed Reaches to Ohio

The river is about 135 miles long and has a watershed of approximately 1,072 square miles, reaching from just south of Jackson on the northwest, just south of Ann Arbor on the north, and into Ohio near the Village of Lyons on the south.

The River Raisin watershed is bordered by the Huron River watershed to the northeast, the watersheds of the Grand and Kalamazoo rivers to the northwest, and the watershed of Ohio's Maumee River which enters Lake Erie near Toledo to the south. (See map on title page.)

At its widest, where it reaches into Ohio on a line between Jackson and Ann Arbor, it is nearly 40 miles north to south. After the river reaches Dundee the watershed narrows to about six miles measured north to south, and for two miles before it reaches Lake Erie it is just over a mile wide. The narrowness at the mouth is caused by several small streams that exit directly into the big lake, Plum and Otter creeks to the south, Mason Run and Sandy Creek to the north.

There are about 450 lakes, both natural and man-created, in the River Raisin watershed area, including several more than one square mile in area.

There are five counties, six cities, ten villages and 40 townships in the watershed. Nearly 65 percent of the land it encloses was zoned for agricultural purposes as late as 2000.

Even the Mouth Meanders

The natural mouth of the River Raisin when settlement began took a decided southerly turn and flowed into Lake Erie about 18 miles north of Toledo through several ponds and winding creeks.

This early port was important because Monroe was also on the route of the first road built in Michigan under the supervision of the Army Engineers and the only port on Lake Erie which was clearly in Michigan Territory. Ohio had become a state in 1805 and claimed that the port at the mouth of the Maumee River, at what would later be called Toledo, was within the political boundaries of the State of Ohio. This question would delay Michigan's bid for statehood by nearly two years and was finally decided in Ohio's favor.

The early port, on La Plaisance Bay, nearly four miles southeast of the community which would later be Monroe, opened onto a bay which was broad and shallow, with a maximum depth for navigation of nine or ten feet. A breakwater was constructed in 1830 to provide a harbor of refuge and to encourage settlement of the extensive agricultural area on the watershed of the River Raisin.. The breakwater was almost completely destroyed by a violent storm in October of 1831.

Instead of extensive repairs on La Plaisance Bay, a new harbor of refuge was proposed in 1834. The mouth of the River Raisin was closed to navigation by an extensive sand flat more than 6,000 feet wide. To overcome this obstacle, a 4,885-foot long canal was proposed from a navigable portion of the River Raisin to Lake Erie, along with perpendicular piers extending into the lake to protect the entrance. This new canal met Lake Erie one and a half miles above the old river mouth. In 1839 engineers recommended that the north pier be extended so it might "serve as a breakwater to the entrance of the channel in times of the severest gales." [2]

River of Sturgeon

The Native Americans called the river Nummasepee or River of Sturgeon, after the number of the large primitive bottom feeding fish they found there.

Some early French maps refer to it as *Riviere aux Ours*, Bear River. It is so designated on DeLisle's *Carte du Canada ou de la Nouvelle France of 1703*, drawn just two years after Detroit was founded. A map published in 1755 by Robert de Vaugondy in Paris labels it *"Ours R."*

The "R aux Ours" on a 1703 French map by DeLisle.

This early map shows the new U. S. Ship Canal built between 1836 and 1842 which runs east from the River Raisin to Lake Erie, but the map also includes the remaining harborworks at La Plaisance Bay. Note also at lower left, the beginning of the tracks for the River Raisin and Lake Erie Railroad which was formed in 1836 to run from La Plaisance Bay to connect with the Erie and Kalamazoo Railroad at Blissfield.

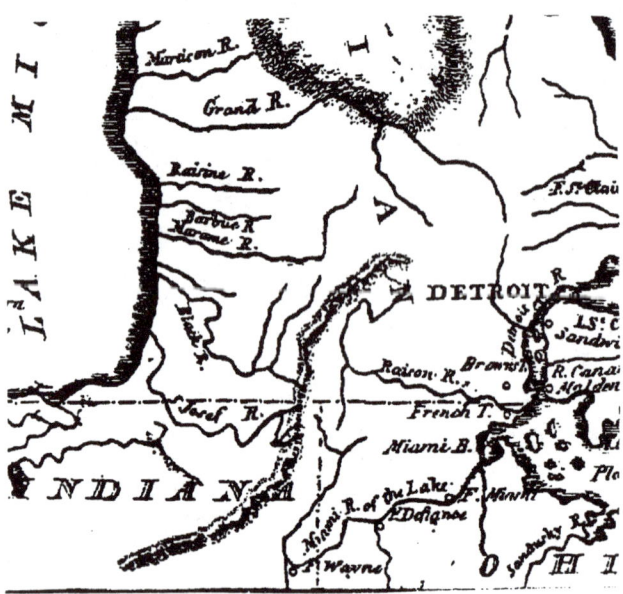

An 1816 map which puts not only the mouth of the Maumee in Ohio, but the mouth of the "Raison" as well. Note also the Raisine R, just south of the Grand River at left.

It is labeled as the "Raison R." on an 1816 map published in Philadelphia by Carey and Warner. Curiously, the cartographer attempted to draw the southern boundary of Michigan according to the provisions of the Northwest Ordinance and shows the settlement of Frenchtown and the mouth of the Raisin both south of the Michigan border in Ohio.

An 1844 map of Lenawee County labels the stream "Riviere Raisin or Grape River."

As late as 1840 there was disagreement about the route of the river. That year a map of the United States engraved by J. H. Young, with Louisiana, Arkansas, Missouri, and Iowa as the nation's western border, clearly shows a river which crosses the lower peninsula of Michigan, from Monroe on Lake Erie through Marshall and into Lake Michigan. It is labeled the Kalamazoo River and appears to be a combination of the Raisin and the Kalamazoo.

Raisins, Raisins everywhere

The grape vines which Blois notes above lined "both banks" were numerous into the 20th Century. The French word for grapes is *"raisin,"* a name reserved in English for dried grapes. In French the river was called *Riviere aux Raisins*, and in deference to the linguistic origins of the name on most maps, even to the present day, it is usually written River Raisin, instead of Raisin River, which is the order more commonly used in English.

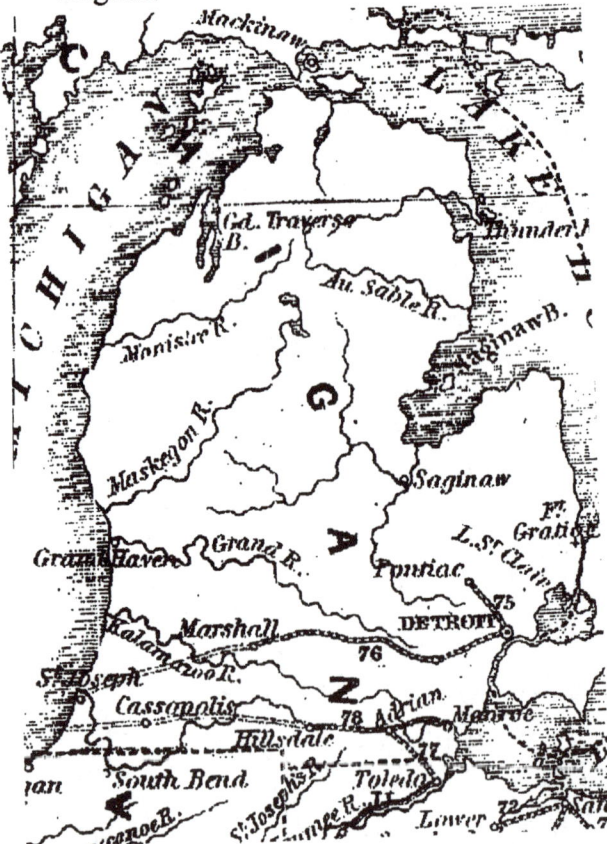

An 1840 map of the United States shows a river which begins at Monroe, passes through Marshall and exits into Lake Michigan. It is labeled Kalamazoo R.

Monroe, February 7, 1819

. . . We have a very pleasant country altho' the ways of the inhabitants are not so agreeable being chiefly French, yet there are many English people daily moving in and the prospect is that many more will move here as soon as the lands are surveyed.

The River Raisin on which we live is a beautiful stream of water about as long again as Mud Creek and abounds with fish of almost every kind. This river lies south of Detroit about 30 miles and is navigable at all seasons about eight miles from its mouth for vessels of about forty tons burthen. In the spring and fall it is navigable fifty miles up it.

The face of the country is very level for twelve miles up the river and timber is chiefly oak and hickory. Above that the land is very different being a great deal higher though not hilly. It is covered with all kinds of timber such as sugar maple, white maple, white wood, basswood, ash, oak hickory, black walnut, butternut, balm of gilead, mulberry and paw paw. There are growing on the bottom lands of this river, five kinds of ash, (to wit) white, black, blue, hoop and prickly ash. The soil of the uplands is of a dark snuff-colored loam and that of the bottom land is a black sand and covered with rushes from two to four feet in length. They are uncommonly thick.

The winters are very light, we have not had more than an inch in depth of snow here this winter and at present there is no frost in the ground, people are all busy about their ploughing. I think I never saw so fine a country for to raise stock in my life. I imagine that there are more than two or three hundred cattle in this place that have not seen a lock of hay or a kernal of corn this winter and they are now good beef.

The old inhabitants are a very indolent set of people, the lower class of which depend almost wholly on hunting for their living. Those of a higher class make great dependence on the fur trade with the indians which is tolerable good at present. Many of the old French settlers have very beautiful orchards in which they raise abundance of apples, pears and cherries which fruit is very natural to this country. There are many inconveniences attending newcomers into this country considering the time it has been settled, the French being very jealous of their rights and likewise very cautious of their dealings with the Yankees as they call all English people, having been many times cheated by many of them.

It is expected that the land will be surveyed and ready for sales in the course of a year – the stated price is two dollars per acre. There is no society here at present except the Roman Catholic. We are in hopes to have a lodge established here shortly and we have some small hopes of having a minister here next summer. In short, if any man has a few extry dollars by him, I think he cannot do better than to lay them out in this country.

                                                  Joseph Bradish

To John B. Bradish
Palmyra, Ontario Co., New York

Once the river had been named Raisin, it became a popular name for settlements and post offices, which must have made mail delivery difficult:

Raisin River was a territorial post office which opened in 1807 somewhere in what would be Monroe County, probably either at the mouth or at Frenchtown.

Raisin was a post office which operated in Lenawee County from 1835 to 1855;

River Raisin PO opened in Washtenaw County in 1864 and closed in 1902.

Raisinville in Monroe County operated as a post office intermittently from 1825 to1842, some of that time being known as **West Raisinville**, before moving west to the village of Hamlin until 1906.

Raisin Center post office operated in Lenawee County from 1868 to 1902. It may have been a revival of the old Raisin post office which has been in existence 1835 to 1855.

Grape, "Raisin" translated, is located on the north bank in Monroe County between Dundee and Monroe. A post office was open there 1887 to 1906.

Navigation, Limited but Useful

An 1819 letter written by Joseph Bradish to relatives in the east boasted that the River Raisin was "navigable at all seasons about eight miles from its mouth for vessels of about forty tons burthen. In the spring and fall it is navigable fifty miles up it."[3]

Eight miles would be about to the community of Raisinville. Fifty miles would be to Floodwood Creek about 10 miles upriver from Deerfield

An 1893 federal report which stated that the River Raisin was "navigable for small craft" 16 miles upriver from the mouth was talking about very small craft. The French farmers used small flat-bottomed bateaux to fish and visit neighbors along the river. The Indians, and the traders when they could get them, used canoes .

Beginning about 1852 a line of steamers was established between Buffalo and Monroe including the **Southern Michigan, the Northern Indiana,** and the **City of Buffalo**, one of the grandest steamboats on the Lakes, but the line was short-lived, replaced by the railroad.

A Great Lakes history of 1899 noted:

> The commerce of Monroe is small, because of the shallowness of the water, and also because of the location between Toledo and Detroit. It is almost entirely limited to receipts of telegraph poles, most of which are brought in rafts with tugs of light draft to tow the rafts in the river. During the warm season of summer several small steamers carry passengers to the small resorts near the mouth. The steamers land at the piers and do not generally run to the Monroe wharves. During the season of 1897, 245 vessels having a registered tonnage of 11,180 arrived, and the same number departed. [4]

Joseph M Sterling built the first shipyard at Monroe's city docks in 1844. Sterling

CITY OF BUFFALO 1896

also planted the first domestic grapevines. The facility at the River Raisin launched its first steamship intended for use on the Great Lakes in 1847, but boatbuilding never became a major industry there.

New Seaway Port Brings Business

New business was brought to the river with the opening of the St. Lawrence Seaway in 1959 taking advantage of Monroe as Michigan's only seaway port on Lake Erie. A 1970 account noted that the new route to the Atlantic Ocean would be a boon to Monroe industry which it listed as: three large paper mills, a tree nursery, Ford Motor Co., Monroe Auto Equipment Co., and a Detroit Edison power plant.

By this time navigation upriver was seriously limited by dams, and the contours of the riverbed, but large ships, from faraway ports had access to docks near the mouth along the canal.

(Above) The City of Buffalo was launched in 1895 for the Cleveland and Buffalo Transit Company and ran between those two cities most of its career. However, old newspapers note several instances when the elegant vessel pulled into the River Raisin with a load of vacationers. The City of Buffalo plied Lake Erie until 1937.

Detroit, July 25, 1803

SIR:

I have endeavored, in the following report, to ascertain and state concisely all those facts concerning which I imagined the Government would wish to be informed. It is little more than an outline, exhibiting the prominent features. The geographical remarks are all made from actual observation; and I have as seldom as the nature of the business would admit depended on the information of others...

Should the report, however, be still defective, if I have omitted the notice of subjects which require investigation, you have only to instruct me, that I may renew my inquiries.

I am your most obedient servant,
C. Jouett, Indian Agent, Detroit

The Honorable Henry Dearborn, Esq., Secretary of the United States for the Department of War

RIVER RAISIN is a delightful stream navigable for small craft about sixteen miles, to the highest farm. It falls into the lake six miles north of Otter Creek, and thirty-six south of Detroit. There are in this settlement one hundred and twenty-one families, who hold their farms by one tenure, namely deeds of bargain and sale from the Pattawatamy, Ottawa, and Chippawa chiefs, executed in the year 1784, 1785 and 1786. The purchasers have been in actual possession since that time. Their farms contain, variously, from one to four hundred French acres, each, fronting on the river from two to six acres and extending back from forty to a hundred and eighty, until they meet the swamps on either side of the river, which serves as a rear boundary for all the farms.

The lands about the mouth of this river are of little value, being too wet for any kind of culture. Those further up are of an excellent soil, producing from twenty-five to thirty bushels to the acre, of wheat, or other grain, in the like proportion. The farms are tolerably well improved, having comfortable dwelling houses, built of hewn logs, and most generally the necessary out-houses such as barns, stables, &c. Their orchards are yet young, but promise in a few years to be very productive. The inhabitants are Canadian French, with only three exceptions. Among these people, disputes have frequently arisen relative to their titles; and those disputes have always terminated by an adjudication in favor of the oldest Indian deed.

They are considered as freeholders, and enjoy every privilege which appertains to a fee simple estate; a number of them holding offices under the territorial Government.

Natives and Early Visitors

Lake Erie was the last of the five Great Lakes to be "discovered" by Europeans. Since the hostile Iroquois controlled the Niagara River, early explorers and traders followed rivers west from Lake Ontario to Georgian Bay on Lake Huron.

There has been considerable speculation for nearly 300 years that Etienne Brule might have crossed a portion of Lake Erie in 1615. Some old sources indicate that two Jesuit missionaries, Father Joseph le Carron and Father Jean de Brebeuf, are the two most often mentioned, paddled up the Raisin searching for native peoples to convert to Christianity in 1634. If the old French notations are properly understood they encountered members of the Chippewa (or Ojibway), Ottawa, Pottawatomi and Wyandotte tribes. If the trip actually occurred, the priests did not stay long; the river visit was just a side trip on a large journey assessing the spiritual needs of inland North America.

The first documented visit by a European to Lake Erie was Adrien Jolliet, said to be the older brother of Louis Jolliet who would later join Father Jacques Marquette in discovery of the Mississippi River. He traveled Lake Erie to Detroit in the summer of 1669. A party headed by Robert Chevalier de la Salle, encountered Jolliet as he was returning in the fall of the same year. Jolliet convinced Father Dollier de Casson and Father Galinee who accompanied LaSalle that there were many prospective converts in the area and offered them maps and use of a canoe he had secreted at the portage and they decided on the Lake Erie trip. LaSalle chose not to accompany the missionaries, but followed rivers and streams to the south. The Sulpician priests hugged the northern shore of Lake Erie as Jolliet had done and probably did not set eyes on the River Raisin, although it is a possibility.

In August of 1679 La Salle in a wooden sailing ship of 60 tons burthen called the **Griffin** (with a suitable figurehead) sailed from Lake Ontario into Lake Erie and up the coast, passing the mouth of the River Raisin then at La Plaisance Bay, and into what was later called the Detroit River. Those aboard marveled at the richness of the country on either side of the passage.

THE GRIFFIN.

The Griffin disappeared in September of 1679 on a fur delivery trip from Green Bay to Niagara. La Salle, who had left the ship in Green Bay, was forced to walk across the Lower Peninsula of Michigan on his way back to Montreal.

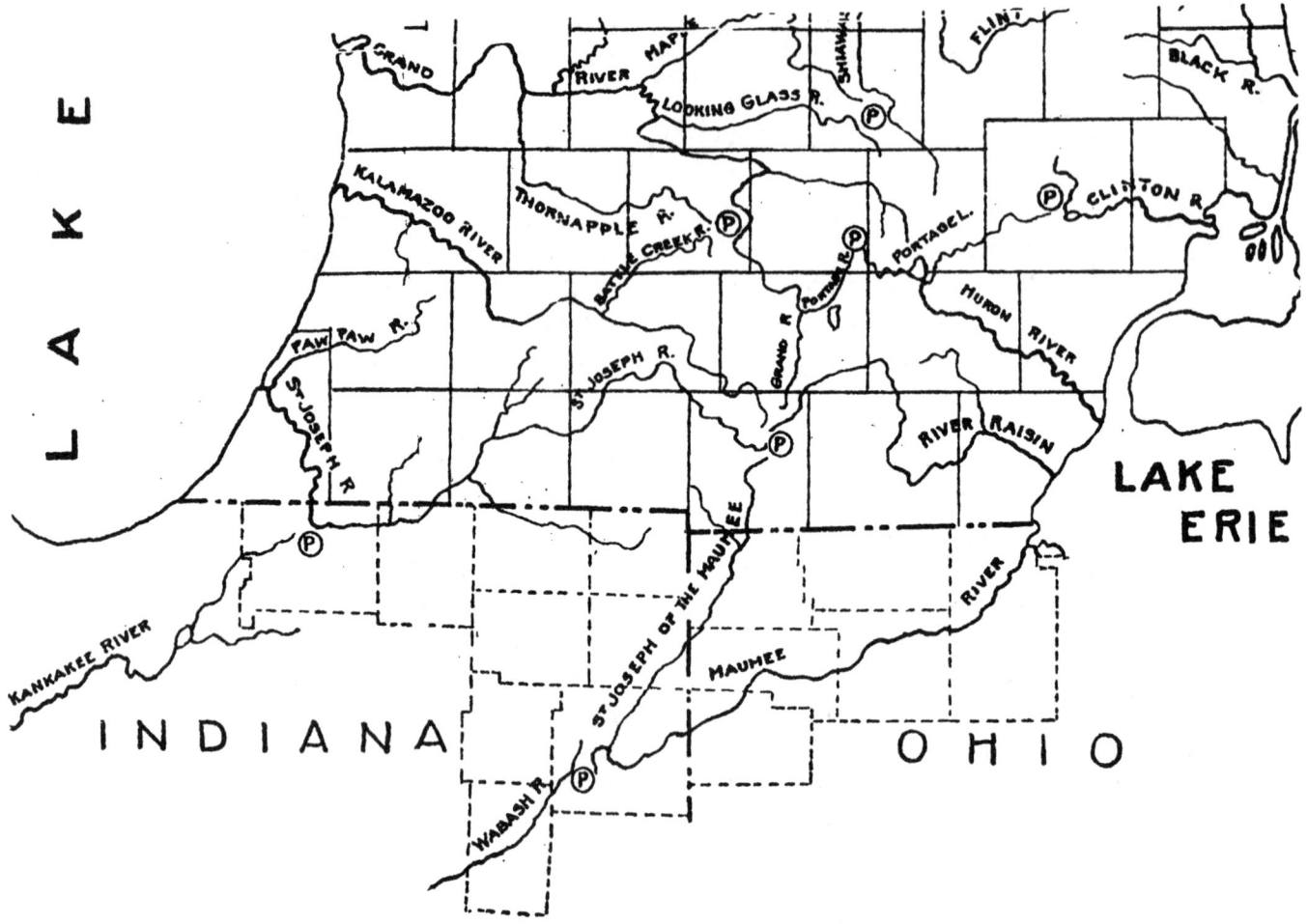

(Above) Indian portages in lower Michigan based on a map in the 1931 archeological atlas by Wilbert Hinsdale.

Father Louis Hennepin, who traveled with LaSalle's party, described the scene:

> The country is very well situated and the soil very fertile. The banks of the strait are vast meadows and the prospect is terminated with some hills covered with vineyards, trees bearing good fruit, groves and forests so well disposed that one would think Nature alone could not have made, without the help of Art, so charming a prospect.[5]

Popular Portages

The River Raisin could be used to go places, but it was so crooked as to make the journey longer, and the portages were not as short or convenient as some on other rivers. It is said that at high water, travelers did not have to unload, or sometimes even leave, their canoes to travel from the Huron into the Grand to cross the lower peninsula. But the salt springs on the Saline River, which enters the Raisin in Monroe County, were a favorite stopping place.

Going upriver into eastern Hillsdale County, there were portages near the great collection of headwaters, of from one-half to three miles, into:

1. The Kalamazoo which empties into Lake Michigan at Saugatuck;

An 1819 map of the Indian reservation on the River Raisin at the intersections of the Macon and Saline rivers. The section lines were added after the first survey, and don't quite match up to the reservation lines on the west.

2. The Grand, via Clark Lake, which reaches Lake Michigan at Grand Haven, Ottawa County;

3. The St. Joseph which has its mouth on Lake Michigan at St. Joseph-Benton Harbor, but which also offered a portage of about four miles into the Kankakee River and thence into the Illinois River and on to the Mississippi;

4. Southward into the Little St. Joseph, or St. Joseph of the Maumee which connected at Ft. Wayne with the Maumee and the Wabash rivers.

Early Reservations

Other old sources record that before white settlement the site of Monroe contained two Indian villages, one Ottawa and one Pottawatomi. Both groups were later forced out of the area by the Iroquois.

A group of Indians living along the River Raisin near the mouth of Macon Creek, was early recognized and a reservation was set apart for them in the treaty of November 17, 1807. It was located near the intersection of the Macon and Raisin rivers near present-day Dundee. The reservation was surveyed by James McCloskey in 1818, before the township grid had been surveyed. He may have tried to anticipate the structure of the townships, if so he missed slightly on the western boundary. The end result is that the main road going north from Dundee follows not the section line, as is customary, but the original boundary line of the old reservation.

A portion of the reservation, about 1817, was ceded to the church and set aside as land on which to build a college. The natives were described as living in "lodges." Saplings were curved and tied to create a dome-shaped framework and the resultant walls were covered with elm bark in the winter for warmth, and woven grass mats in the summer allowing cool breezes to blow through.

On September 19, 1827, in a treaty concluded at St. Joseph, the remaining portion of the old reservation was ceded to the federal government except for 320 acres north of the River Raisin which was given to Macon, described as a Pottawatomi chief. This smaller reservation was active until 1865.

"Slightly Civilized and Industrious"

The Indians were a source of amazement to the earliest settlers, and probably the reverse was true. Elizabeth Margaret Chandler who arrived at a homestead in 1830 along the river between Tecumseh and Adrian wrote an aunt in June of 1831:

> We have not yet had any Indian visitors, have seen only two since our arrival at Hazelbank. 'Tis said they disposed of the greater part of their horses last fall in their expectation of an unusually severe winter. . . . I went with brother last first day evening to look at their burial mound which is a short distance from here. It had apparently been opened for there was a square cavity at the top and the earth about it looked fresher than below, but I do not think any curiosities have been discovered in any near here that have been examined.

Whiskey, or more commonly "firewater," a concoction of a little whiskey, lots of water given a more pronounced "bite" with the addition of pepper, was often supplied to the natives by the traders. A drunken Indian was a poor businessman, and "firewater" was less expensive than trade goods although it was specifically prohibited in most traders' permits. Margaret Chandler continues in the letter to her aunt:

> When Comstock first came here the Indians were often at their house and on one occasion one of them, who was already half intoxicated after soliciting Darius in vain for liquor, or the means of procuring some, offered to sell his child, a little girl who was with him to friend Comstock for a few dollars opining him that she was "plenty good papoose!" But I think it probable that after his fit was over he would have remanded her, or wished to purchase her back when he was able to do so. [6]

The art with which the native peoples coped with the hardships of their way of life was also admired by many of the newcomers. A 1909 Lenawee County history described the Indians the first white settlers met as, "A powerful race of slightly civilized and industrious people."[7]

Relics of the Mound Builders

There were also mounds and other relics of even more ancient native inhabitants.

Francis A. Dewey, in a book of memoirs, wrote about earthworks found by early settlers on the banks of the River Raisin in Lenawee County near Brownsville (later part of Tecumseh):

> Here was a square enclosure with an embankment of earth four feet high and three rods square with

two openings. Here in this enclosure tradition of the older Indians points with majestic pride, and says there is where the celebrated or imperial chiefs held council. Also near by, on this level and beautiful plat of ground, was a circular embankment or enclosure, four feet high and about two rods in diameter, with a cavity scooped out in the center. Where tradition of olden time illustrates the historical emblems, the sacred plants and herbs were placed in the center of the circle and set on fire; from the fumes of this smoke the pipe of peace or war was dictated by the chiefs to the Indian nations.[8]

Another View of the Mound

With a historical archeologist's view Wilbert Hinsdale later gathered comments from old settlers and described the site:

> In the north part of the City of Tecumseh, near the bank of the River Raisin, at what was once known as Brownsville, there was a circle joined by a passageway to a square. Accurate descriptions of this construction have been left by early observers. A hundred years ago there were still standing the remains of cedar posts so arranged as to indicate that the embankments were palisaded. In the center of the circle a number of pits, five or six feet deep, contained charcoal and firewood. Nearby another circular inclosure was situated and also a "dance circle" a little farther to the northeast.[9]

Dewey, in his description, went on to comment: "Since the year 1832 the plow and cultivator have leveled the historic work of the mound builders." The editors of the memoirs, however, hastened to explain, "The ruthless leveling of the mounds has not been perpetrated, however, merely to gratify the iconoclastic propensities of the ploughman ... they wanted the corn the mounds would produce."

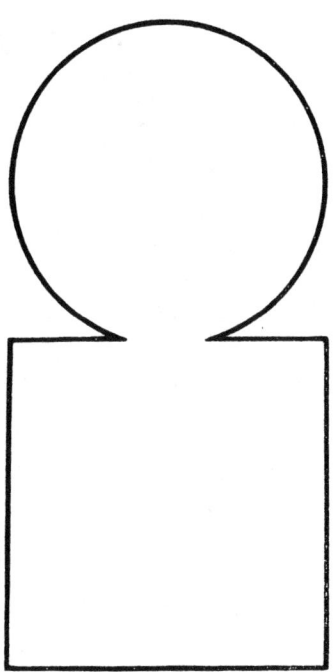

FIG. 13. Diagram showing outline of inclosures, with circle and square connected. Tecumseh

(Above) Diagram based on the description in Hinsdale atlas.

17

Deed by Pottawattamie chiefs to Piere Labady
(translated by Rudolph Worck and Dr. F. Krusty, Editors "Michigan Volksfreund")

We, the chiefs of the Pottawatamies Nation of the Detroit after having deliberated upon the actual state of the lands which we leave uncultivated since long, with the advice and consent of, and in the name of the entire nation have determined to give a portion thereof to our friend Pierre Labady, containing three arpents front on the River Raisin at the right in ascending the said river and maintaining the same depth as the other lands heretofore given away up to a hundred arpents adjacent to the said lands on one side, down the river, is that of Mr. Jean Baptiste Lanserainte and on the other side up the river, that of the widow lady of Alexis Campeau, and for the good friendship, which we bear him, we light for him a fire of peace and tranquillity warranting to him from now and forever

    -- the said piece of land herein presented that he may enjoy it without any hindrance whatever. For this purpose we have made our accustomed mark on the 15th day of May 1786.

Early Settlers

It was not until 1701 that the first true settlement was begun at Detroit. That year Antoine de la Mothe Cadillac arrived to build a military outpost for the French government. A census ordered of the settlement in 1782 counted about 2,300 inhabitants. These citizens were nearly all of French extraction but by that year their political status was less clear.

Britain Takes Over

The French and Indian War which officially began in 1756, as part of a worldwide struggle between France and England, ended with a British victory. In the Treaty of Paris, concluded in 1763, French citizens who were resident in areas of North America awarded to Britain, such as Detroit, were allowed to keep their lands, their homes and their religion. Little changed in their way of life. The main language of the Detroit area was French, the residents still raced little French ponies on the streets of the city and they lived on ribbon farms, which had a narrow frontage on the riverbank and ran back from the river for sometimes up to a mile.

The political status of the citizens who lived in what would become Michigan was confused even more by the American Revolution. When the war ended with the Treaty of Ghent in 1783, all of Michigan was still in British hands, but the land was not surveyed, and the American government and military were so concerned with problems in the east of the new country that the British garrison stayed on at Detroit and Mackinac Island until 1796.

This set of circumstances meant that, although the French (by lineage, tradition and language) inhabitants of Detroit and the River Raisin valley were legally American citizens, they were living under British rule.

Moving South

Fortunately New World Frenchmen of that era did not worry much about politics. About 1780 the best lands in the Detroit area had been taken and farmers, often in family groups, began to move into other river valleys in the southeast corner of the peninsula. One of the most promising rivers, overgrown with wild grapes, was the one they called *Riviere aux Raisins* or the River Raisin. Since the land was not yet surveyed the settlers purchased it from the Indians, or were sometimes the recipients of free grants from them.

Navarre First Settler

The first white man to spend time on the River Raisin was fur trader Joseph Pulier, but the first true settler was Francois Navarre, who built a trader's cabin in 1780. Navarre had served as an interpreter for General Lewis Cass. His son was the first white child born in the valley of the River Raisin and it is recorded that he planted French pear trees on the banks of the river in 1786.

Navarre was followed shortly by Charles and John Baptiste Jerome. By 1803 about a hundred French families, mostly from Canada, had settled on the north bank of the Raisin, reaching nearly 15 miles upriver. The community was called Frenchtown and was only the third permanent settlement in what would later be Michigan, after only Detroit and Mackinac.

Since the land had not been surveyed, and at the beginning of settlement, the governmental jurisdiction was not clear, the only way to "purchase" any kind of worthwhile title was from the Indians who lived there. In some cases land was given to specific settlers as a gift, with the approval of the "chiefs." The deeds were usually written out in French, signed and witnessed with the Native Americans sealing the agreement with their names transliterated into English accompanied by their mark or clan symbols.

"Tolerably Well Improved"

In 1803, C Jouett, an Indian agent from Detroit, reported (apparently by request) to Henry Dearborn, President Thomas Jefferson's Secretary of State, that the River Raisin was, "a delightful stream navigable for small craft about sixteen miles." He counted 121 families living on the banks of the river and notes, "The inhabitants are Canadian French, with only three exceptions." Jouett describes the farms as "tolerably well improved."

Records of Michigan Territory, formed in 1805 after Ohio became a state, indicate that there was a post office called Raisin River opened in 1807 in the area of the territory which later became Monroe County. Moses Morse was the first postmaster, succeeded by Colonel John Anderson. This may have been a "stage coach" office, where mail was dropped as the stage came through on its way to Detroit. In 1815 an official federal post office opened in the settlement, the second in Michigan Territory, preceded only by the post office at Detroit.

Even with an American post office the settlers on the River Raisin were still very French in their ways and were looked on with disdain by "Yankees." New Yorker Edward D. Ellis wrote in 1829:

> The early settlers were of a class and description almost entirely devoid of enterprise. They, like many of their offspring, were content with seating themselves upon the fertile banks of the rivers, watching in sullen silence the fish as they glided in the waters, and cultivated their lands barely sufficient to supply their immediate wants.[10]

A settler who arrived in 1823 wrote that the French inhabitants "dressed more like Indians than white people. Farming was done in the most primitive style. The oxen were broken to draw by their horns, and instead of wagons they used horse carts, without tire or a particle of iron about them. There was only one wagon ironed off in the county, and that was left here by the army of 1812."[11]

After the War

Frenchtown was nearly abandoned after the War of 1812, and in 1817 an American settlement was platted on the south bank of the river and named for newly-elected president, James Monroe. To link the two settlements John Anderson, Oliver Johnson and 12 others

BRICK WALKER TAVERN, R.F.D. BROOKLYN, MICHIGAN

(Above) The three-story brick tavern owned by Sylvester Walker at Cambridge Junction. This postcard shows a slightly idealized depiction of the area in the late 1800s.

were authorized to build a toll bridge across the River Raisin. The bridge washed out by ice flows on March 6, 1832.

Most of the non-French settlements up the river were created during the 1820s, and received an additional economic boost in 1878 when the Lake Shore & Michigan Southern Railroad was constructed with much of the route along the River Raisin valley.

Dundee was first settled in 1824 by Riley Ingersoll from New York State. The first dam, built of brush, was constructed in 1827 to power a sawmill.

Tecumseh was founded in 1824 by Musgrove Evans, Joseph W. Brown and Austin E. Wing. It was Lenawee County seat from 1826 to 1837.

Petersburg was originally the farm of Richard Peters who came to that area of Monroe County in 1824. Thomas G. Cole and Austin E. Wing founded the village on land acquired from Peters in 1836.

Kedzie First in Two Towns

William Kedzie of New York, made the first government land purchase at

Blissfield in May of 1824, but he did not settle in the area until the fall of 1826. Hervey Bliss, from Monroe County, was the first settler, arriving in December of 1824.

Kedzie was also responsible for the settlement at Deerfield, (15 miles downstream) at about the same time. The town was first called Kedzie's Grove.

An Early Crossroads

In 1826 the federal government began work on a Detroit to Chicago road. It was largely built on the Old Sauk Trail, an Indian pathway, and is similar to the highway which was later U.S. 12. Ten years later a private company built a road from La Plaisance Bay on Lake Erie to Jackson. The two roads crossed at Cambridge Junction south of Vineyard Lake in Lenawee County and the very beginnings of the Raisin River pass through the settlement.

A tavern was built in 1836 at the crossroads, and purchased in 1843 by Sylvester S. Walker. In 1853 he constructed a three-story brick tavern across the road. The smaller frame tavern was acquired by the Michigan Department of Natural Resources in 1965 and is now Cambridge Junction State Historic Park.

Palmyra was founded in 1827 by Timothy B. Goff, and named for his hometown in New York.

Clinton, Lenawee county, was settled by John Terrill and Thaddeus Clark in 1830, the first post office opening in 1831.

Upriver towns were later in development. Norvell, Jackson County, was first settled in 1831 by William Hunt.

The first land claim in Brooklyn, Jackson county, was filed by Calvin H. Swaine, in 1832. The following year he built a sawmill. The settlement was earlier called Swainesville.

Manchester, Washtenaw County, was part of a grant to Major John Gilbert in 1833 who platted the town, but the first settlers were James Harvey Fargo, and his uncle Steven Fargo, proprietors of the Manchester Mill Company. Gilbert built the first mill in 1833, and a pole bridge was erected across the River Raisin at Main Street.

War of 1812

The military action which began in 1812 between the fledgling United States of America and Britain is sometimes called the Second War of Independence. It is more commonly referred to as the War of 1812, even though it actually lasted from June 18, 1812, until the Treaty of Ghent, signed December 24, 1814.

"Free Trade and Sailors' Rights"

England's repeated impressment of American citizens to fight on British ships in its war against France was the most visible reason for the conflict.

Also related to the British-French war was Napoleon's 1806 decree declaring all commerce with Great Britain by any nation illegal, and the British government's answering Orders in Council which forbade commerce with continental ports unless the ship first called at a British port and paid appropriate duties. In protest against this affront to its shipping America passed the Embargo Act which prohibited ALL American exports to ANY country. The rallying cry of the conflict was "Free Trade and Sailors' Rights."

British Behind Indian Problems

The underlying causes of the war were more subtle. There was a growing feeling in America that the British in Canada were intentionally keeping the Indians riled up against the American settlers to the point of actually supplying arms. Several senators expressed the idea in Congress that the Indians could not be controlled until the new country first eliminated the Spanish in Florida and the British in Canada. There was also a land lust on both sides. Some Americans wanted to expand into Canada, and the British wanted their former colonies back under the Union Jack.

On June 18, 1812, war against Britain was formally declared in Washington. However the news did not reach Michigan until July 2. William Hull, who had been appointed Michigan's first territorial governor in 1805, was on his way back from Washington where he had gone to ask for aid. Instead he had been appointed commander of all of the operations in the West, with the rank of brigadier general.

Mackinac Island Falls

On July 17, 1812, British soldiers captured the fort on Mackinac Island, and thus controlled the trade routes of the upper Great Lakes. On July 28 all occupants of Fort Dearborn (where Chicago later stood), military, civilian and a band of friendly Miami Indians, began to withdraw to Fort Wayne, Indiana, to seek greater protection. A mile and a half from the fort they were attacked by a band of Indians. More than 90 people who started the march died in the battle before most of the others surrendered and were taken captive.

One of the first projects completed by General Hull in Michigan was a supply road from the south to Detroit which passed through Frenchtown on the River Raisin. A detachment of volunteers from

The log cabin home of Francois Navarre, along the banks of the River Raisin. He planted the first French pear trees in the county.

Francois Navarre

The first settler on the Raisin was born in Detroit about 1760 and first visited the River Raisin in 1780, returning in 1784 to settle.

In 1785 he received a deed for about 1200 acres, most of downtown Monroe, from the Indians, some say it was the result of a dream which he related to the chief. It was the tradition of the Indians to honor dreams. The chief then warned him that he needed to stop dreaming.

He acted as an interpreter during the 1795 Indian treaty at Greenville assisting General Anthony Wayne.

When the first militia outside of the Detroit area was formed he was made a Captain and then a Colonel. Navarre served in most of the early political offices and was made Justice of the County Court. He was host to General Winchester during the War of 1812 battles.

Francois (sometimes anglicized to Francis) and his wife, Marie Suzor, had seven sons and five daughters. Francois died in 1826. The surname of Navarre is still common in Monroe County today

Ohio had used the road to bring provisions for the army and had requested an escort to Detroit, but the escort, heading south to connect with the supply train, was attacked at the Ecorse River and retreated.

Hull Surrenders Detroit

On August 16 a large force of British regular troops and Indians landed on the Detroit side of the river and called on Hull to surrender, warning of the danger of Indian massacre if there was resistance. Hull not only surrendered Detroit, but included verbiage in the surrender document which included "a detachment from the State of Ohio on its way to join his Army" and the provisions for the army which had been assembled at the River Raisin.

The son of a British Indian agent was sent to Frenchtown with word of the surrender, but he was detained on the road by friendly militia and most of the Ohio troops, along with their stores of supplies, escaped successfully back to Ohio.

A force of British soldiers was dispatched to Frenchtown along with some Indian allies. The British military men burned Fort Wayne, a blockhouse which had been built on the north bank of the river west of the main part of the settlement (near the later intersection of Elm and Monroe streets). The Indians, according to one early historian, "ravaged the settlement without restraint." [12]

Kentucky Responds to the Call

The settlers in Kentucky, who had experienced more Indian troubles than many of the older cities to the east, were eager to volunteer for wartime service. After war was declared the quotas were rapidly filled, and on August 12 a regiment formed almost entirely of men from Franklin County, Kentucky, rendezvoused at Newport on the Ohio River and began to move north rapidly, hampered considerably by a lack of supplies, arms and uniforms (most importantly proper footwear).

After crossing the river they passed through Lebanon, Dayton, Piquot, and Fort Wayne, before turning largely east up the Maumee River valley. On January 10, 1813, the regiment arrived at Fort Defiance on the Maumee River in Ohio near where Toledo was later founded.

North on the Ice

On January 13 two Frenchmen arrived at the camp from the River Raisin and reported to the commander of the Kentucky troops, Brigadier General James Winchester, that their presence was known to the British and Indian forces, and that this information had been sent on to the headquarters at Fort Malden, across the river and south of Detroit in Canada. Two days later another Monroe County resident arrived imploring protection for the people and property on the River Raisin. On January 17 another man came with the news that the British had arrived from Canada and the Indians were collecting and intended to burn Frenchtown shortly.

Bowing to the cause, a detachment of 550 men under Colonel William Lewis left early January 17, marching northward. Part of the route was along the shore of the frozen lake. When they arrived at the mouth of the Raisin about noon on January 18 they met residents of Frenchtown fleeing the community. The

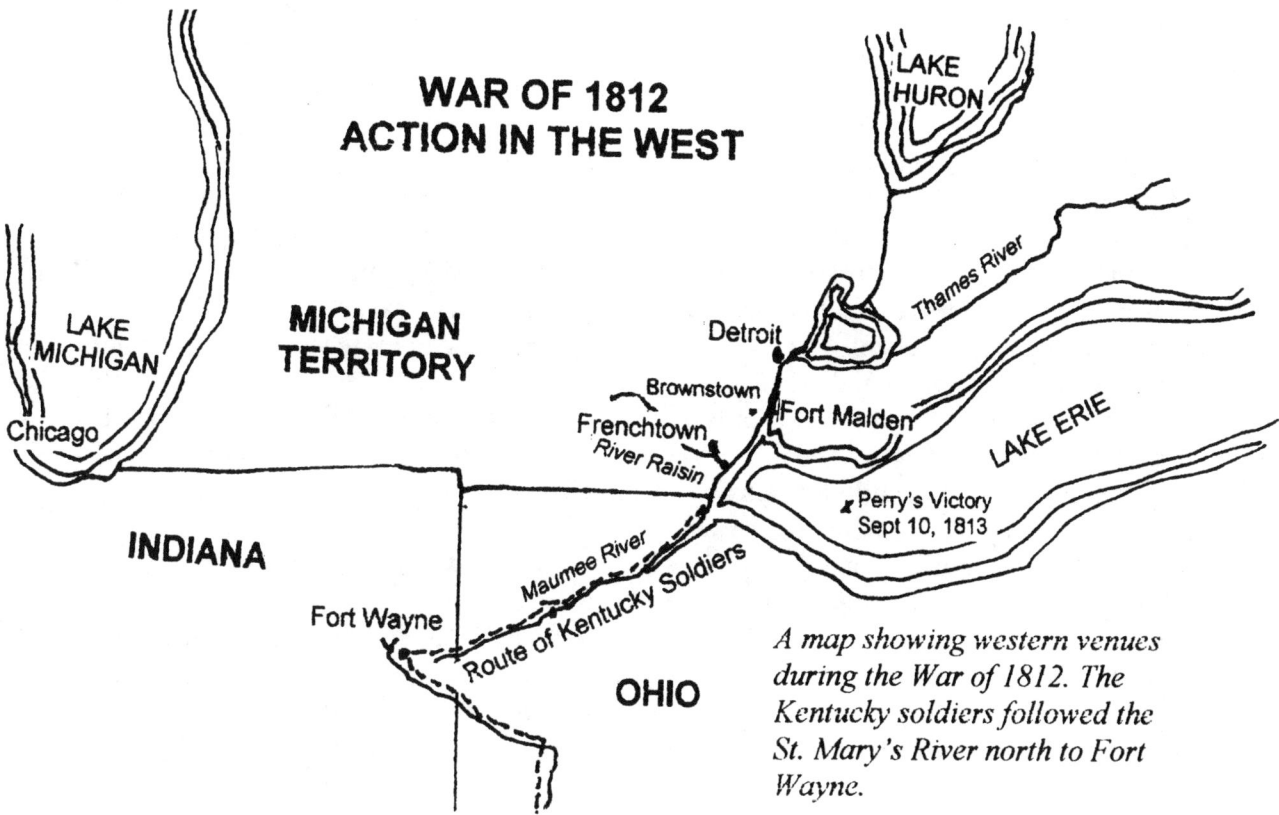

A map showing western venues during the War of 1812. The Kentucky soldiers followed the St. Mary's River north to Fort Wayne.

troops asked if the British had any artillery and were told, "They have two pieces about large enough to kill a mouse."

Dogs, Chickens and Mice

About three o'clock the American soldiers began crossing the frozen Raisin and, according to an eyewitness, on reaching the opposite shore "raised a yell, some crowing like chicken cocks, some barking like dogs, and others calling, 'Fire away with your mouse cannon again.'" [13]

Gradually the British and Indians were pushed back to the woods on the northern edge of the settlement. The fighting raged for three hours, and about dusk officers were sent to stop the pursuit of the enemy and the troops were told to return to Frenchtown bearing the killed for burial and the wounded for treatment. The Americans buried 13 dead, all except one had been scalped.

All was quiet for a few days. General Winchester, with an additional 200 Kentuckians reached Frenchtown on the 20th. The troops were camped in and around buildings on the north bank, most behind a puncheon fence that marked the settlement's garden. General Winchester was bivouacked snugly in the home of Francois Navarre on the south side of the river. In retrospect there was much criticism for this choice of lodging, away from his men. However, Winchester was not well-liked, in training camp sabotaging his latrine was a favorite activity, so he probably felt more secure away from the enlisted men.

On the 22nd just as reveille was sounding the first gun was fired. The troops on the north side of the river dressed hurriedly and began at once to organize for battle. Across the river Francois Navarre went upstairs to rouse General Winchester who left the house so quickly that he left his uniform coat behind.

The men behind the garden fence were holding their own, but the regulars were falling back toward the river. Several militia men, including Colonel Allen were lost trying to go to their aid.

Barefoot in the Snow

Other Kentuckians retreated safely about three miles to the south where they were overtaken. A least two soldiers, finding the Indians closing in, pulled off their shoes and ran Indian fashion through the snow so as to leave tracks which looked like they were made by Indians. Both eventually escaped and returned to the military base at the rapids on the Maumee River.

General Winchester, on horseback, was captured by Indians. Shortly after, fire slackened and then nearly ceased except for stray shots from the Indian scouts. Their portion of the battle had been going so well that American soldiers, behind the garden fence were beginning to think that the silence meant another American victory. They were surprised to see a white flag being brought by one of their own.

An Answering White Flag

A second flag of truce was brought by those behind the fence including Major George Madison so that they could parlay with the first flag bearer. When he approached the flag the British commander, Colonel Henry A. Proctor, appeared and gave the same ultimatum which had been given to General Hull at Detroit. He warned the American officers that unless the entire force surrendered the Indians could not be restrained from murdering all of them, the wounded and the fighting alike. The Americans also, for the first time, heard the news that General Winchester had been captured and was ordering the surrender.

Madison was angry at the surrender when it seemed, from a military standpoint, that the Americans had the upper hand. He also expressed misgivings that "it was customary for the Indians to massacre the wounded prisoners." He said he could not agree to any surrender unless the safety and protection of the men were secured.

Terms of Surrender

After a good deal of discussion, and a consultation with wounded officers warily watching the whole procedure from their makeshift hospital ward in nearby cabins, surrender terms were arranged and agreed upon by both Madison and the British. All private property was to be respected, sleds would be sent the following morning to transport the wounded to Amherstburg and there would be guards left at Frenchtown until that could be accomplished.

While the men were still talking a group of Indians crowded around and began help themselves to the soldiers' clothing and personal effects. When the Americans appealed to a British officer he at first said, "The Indians

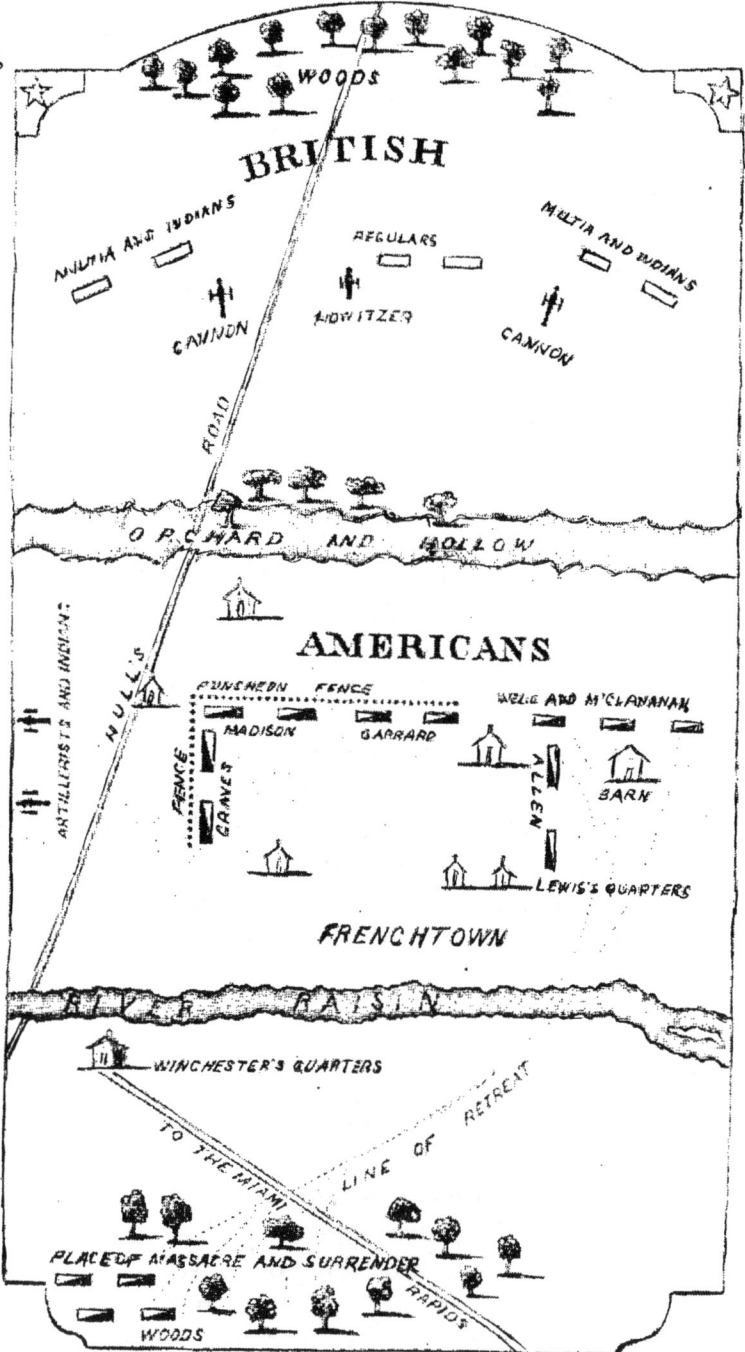

This map, which shows the grounds of the battle on both sides of the River Raisin in January of 1813 and the position of the military units for American and British troops, was found among British army papers and is thought to have been drawn by, or at the direction of, General Proctor for a military tribunal.

are fierce and unmanageable, it cannot be done." But he later waved the natives off with his sword and they withdrew.

British Leave in a Hurry

The surrender concluded, the British, in considerable haste, fearing the arrival of reinforcements for the American troops, left for Fort Malden near Amherstburg with the American prisoners of war and the walking wounded.

The British left two cabins full of wounded, including several of their own men. Some of the soldiers had been in the make shift hospital since the first battle on January 18. British Captain William Elliot, who had visited Kentucky, was the officer in charge of the wounded. He was left behind with three Indian interpreters, but shortly after nightfall Elliot took a horse belonging to a wounded soldier and disappeared into the night.

The Indians attacked with the first light of dawn.

Were Indians Intoxicated?

There has been speculation about whether the natives were drunk that morning. They had been promised a "victory celebration" at Stoney Point, on Lake Erie to the north, and many felt the British had supplied the strong drink. One of the survivors wrote that Colonel John Anderson had a trading post near the banks of the river and when he heard that General Winchester had been captured took steps to keep drink out of the hand of the Indians.

Knowing well the barbarous habits and customs of the savages, especially when under the influence of liquor, he hurried to the cellar of his store where his liquors were stored, and knocked in the heads of his whisky barrels, and then concealed himself under the plates of a neighboring barn for nearly two days. The Indians burst in the door, ransacked his store, then prostrated themselves on their breasts in the cellar and filled themselves with whiskey.[14]

Dr. John Todd who had been up all night attending the wounded testified afterwards that he didn't think the Indians were drunk, only very angry at the number of their own who had been killed in battle. "Whiskey, was not the cause of the massacre," he stated. "Their deliberate pilfering and their orderly conduct throughout was not such as would be expected from a drunken Indian."[15]

Records are not clear whether these Indians were the same ones who participated in the battle on January 22. One writer explained that they were "not Tecumseh's people, but Indians of the Lake, prowlers and plunderers." Most sources agree that they were probably Iroquois.[16]

Tomahawks and Fire

The Indians began by crowding into the two buildings and removing articles and items of clothing from the wounded, followed by a tomahawk to the head, tossing the body out onto the snow. When they had all of the goods they desired they went outside and set fire to the two buildings. Wounded men who managed to struggle to the door or

A small monument erected on the site of the main battle by the "Women of Monroe" in 1904. It now sits in Riviere aux Raisin Park at Elm Street and Dixie Highway.

window to escape were tomahawked, or tossed back into the flames.

Some of the men were claimed as prisoners by individuals and marched off in various directions. Others formed a line set to march on to Brownstown, and eventually it was assumed, to Fort Malden. Those who could not keep up were tomahawked, others were killed indiscriminately.

The dead were left along the road and the bodies at Frenchtown were left in the burned buildings and on the ground where they had fallen. The Indians promised quick reprisal to any who dared to attempt to bury them.

Prisoners on to Niagara

The prisoners who actually reached Fort Malden were sent on to a prison at Niagara where parole was arranged and each man left to find his own way home. Some of those taken prisoner by the Indians were never heard from again, others were ransomed by friendly Detroiters.

For more than a year after the battle Kentucky soldiers straggled home. In Franklin County a cannon was fired each time a survivor arrived and all within sound of the shot would hurry to town to greet the returned soldier and inquire after those still missing. Major George Madison did not arrive in Frankfort until May 4, 1814. Two years later he was elected governor of Kentucky.

The War of 1812 continued, the Americans buoyed by Admiral Oliver Hazard Perry's victory on Lake Erie in September of 1813. In the midwest the British finally left Detroit in late September, having burned many of the new public buildings which had been constructed following Detroit's great fire of 1805.

The British retreated to Canada and began moving up the Thames River valley. In hot pursuit a force of 5,500 men left Fort Meigs on the Maumee in late September. When they crossed the River Raisin on the way to Detroit they found the mutilated bodies from the January battles still lying on the ground, body parts being spread over a large area by wild hogs and other animals. One historian commented: "The grisly scene had an effect on the Kentuckians more profound than any exhortation *[Colonel Richard Mentor]* Johnson or *[William Henry]* Harrison himself might have delivered."

Remember the Raisin!

The memory of what happened on the River Raisin became an important rallying cry for the American forces. According to a 1903 account:

> When the final charge was made against General Henry A. Proctor across the swampland adjoining the Thames the tense stillness of impending combat was upon the Americans. But when the "Forward. Charge!" order echoed through the ranks another cry, terrible in its intensity and with foreboding wrath in its tones, filled the space overshadowed by the mighty monarchs of the forest. From the stalwart throats of nearly six hundred Kentuckians there arose the cry, "Remember the Raisin!" As they lifted this mighty cry to Heaven they saw about them the forms of their murdered comrades and friends and relatives. . . As the cry of these Kentuckians resounded through the forests, it fell upon the ears of British regulars, who themselves had been at the battle of the Raisin, and whose officers had connived at, or at least permitted the slaughter. . . . In the fierce charge there was but one cry, oft repeated, but rising each time in sharper and sterner tones, "Remember the Raisin! Remember the Raisin!"[17]

On October 5, 1813, the American force caught up with the British troops near Moraviantown, along the Thames River about 50 miles east of Detroit in Canadian territory. Tecumseh was killed in that battle, although the body was so mutilated that it was difficult to be certain which corpse was his.

A Proper Burial at Last

On October 15, 1813, on the way home from the battle on the Thames, a group of Kentucky soldiers stopped long enough to gather the remains of those killed at Frenchtown and bury them in a common grave. They figured that they had found the major portion of 65 bodies. Some were later moved to cemeteries in Detroit and Kentucky.

In remembrance of the Kentucky participants in what was later known as the River Raisin Massacre, the State of Kentucky, between 1815 and 1825 named nine newly-formed counties to honor Colonel John Allen, Major Benjamin F. Graves, and Captains Bland W. Ballard, John M. Edmonson (or Edmiston), Nathaniel F. S. Hart, Paschal Hickman, Virgil McCracken, James Meade and John Simpson, defenders of Frenchtown.

At the time of the burial in 1813, there were no residents of the town of Frenchtown in view. Talcott Wing wrote in 1883:

> So intolerable was the annoyance and danger, the Americans with their families fled to Ohio and

(Above) Michigan's "tribute to Kentucky" dedicated in 1904.

Kentucky, the French settlers to Canada, and for the following three years, this portion of the State was deserted . . . . One after another of the families in 1816, '17, and '18, returned to Frenchtown.

Old Soldiers Gather

During a solemn parade in 1872 a group of old Kentucky soldiers halted at the site on Monroe Avenue between 6th and 7th streets where the remains of those killed had been buried. General George A. Custer, a member of the local welcoming committee, read the roll call of the veterans.

Before the close of the reunion residents of Monroe had promised "to erect a monument to the memory of the chivalrous heroes. . . who marched at the call of our distressed little settlement and laid down their lives as a sacrifice in its behalf."[18]

The ladies of the Monroe Civic Improvement Society encouraged the city to established the old burial ground as a park. In 1903 State Senator Simeon Van Akin introduced a bill in the Legislature to fund the project and the monument was formally dedicated in September of 1904.

Prominent in the dedicatory ceremonies was an "historic flag" carried in the parade which was attached to a staff which had been made from timbers of the house which had been occupied by General James Winchester, commander of the Kentucky troops in 1813. The flag and staff had also been carried by Monroe troops in the Civil War and the Spanish American War. A major address was given by Michigan Governor Aaron T. Bliss.

The large granite monument reads:

> Michigan's tribute to Kentucky.
> This monument is dedicated to the memory of the heroes who
> lost their lives in our country's defense at the
> battle and massacre
> of the River Raisin
> January 22nd and 23rd, 1813
> Erected by the State of Michigan
> -- 1904 --

At 1403 East Elm Street, near the battlefield, the local historical society converted an old residence into the River Raisin Battlefield Center, with exhibits relating to the battle, and a fiber optic map presentation of the movements. The center is open April to September. In addition, an annual commemoration ceremony marking the anniversary of the massacre is held in January on the weekend closest to January 22.

National Battlefield Planned

In 2006 a bill was enacted in Congress to study the possibility of designating the old Frenchtown site, now a part of the City of Monroe, as a National Battlefield.

The following year, to help the process along, the State of Michigan and local organizations put together $2.25 million to demolish a former paper mill which would clear a major portion of the site.

Just across the street from the paper mill ruins, there is a second monument shown on a 1904 postcard on the banks of the River Raisin which reads:

> Site of battles of January 19-22, 1813,
> Gen. Winchester in command
> and River Raisin massacre
> January 23, 1813
>
> Erected 1904
> by the Civic Improvement Society
> of the Women of Monroe.

This monument is now at the Monroe city park on Elm Street and the Dixie Highway called Riviere aux Raisin Park, which will be developed as part of the National Battlefield project.

Floods and Bridges

The first recorded flood on the River Raisin occurred on April 8, 1836. The scene was described in an 1881 history:

> For several days previous it had been quite warm and pleasant. All nature seemed to wear the cheerfulness of spring. The roads had become dry and passable after the frosts of winter, when, unexpectedly, the sky began to darken and the rain to descend in torrents. The storm continued with slight intermission, for about 12 hours. The effects were such as probably never before had been witnessed in this county. Little rivulets by the wayside were swollen into large streams, tearing up the roads, sweeping away crossways, bridges and fences. The larger streams and rivers arose with corresponding rapidity, continuing and extending the work of destruction on a more magnificent scale. The roads on all sides were rendered almost impassable, while many of the most important bridges on the main roads were swept away and machinery on the different streams was more or less damaged.[19]

With water sometimes came fire. The first sawmill in Sharon Township was built on section 20 by Amasa Gilett and B. F. Burnett on the extreme northerly bend of the River Raisin. The running gear of the mill was placed above the saw and, according to ear witnesses, made a terrible noise. Later the friction produced by this gear set fire to the wood and destroyed the mill.[20]

Manchester Loses a Dam in 1875

After a hard winter in 1875 April arrived to find thick ice on the river just breaking up and beginning to move downstream. On April 1 at Lansing the pack ice took out five iron bridges that spanned the Grand River in one day. At Manchester along the Raisin the bridge held but the dam went out. The April 8, 1875, *Manchester Enterprise* describes the scene:

> Our Citizens were startled on Friday forenoon by the rushing noise of the river at the dam, and many hastened to the bridge to see what was up, when all at once the dam gave way and the water went rushing down the stream, bearing upon its bosom large cakes of ice, timbers, floodwood, etc. The pressure was so great upon the bridge that it was feared that it too would be lost, but it withstood the pressure and came out all safe, only in a very dilapidated condition. In a very short time people were allowed to gaze upon the bed of the river, a sight but few now living have every beheld. The great amount of water bore away the bulk-head of the floom *[flume?]* at the tannery dam but did no further serious damage. The news flew like wildfire and a large crowd of people were upon

the spot viewing the wreck. The boys availed themselves of the opportunity and hundreds of fish, both large and small, soon fell prey to the excited throng. The river has never had such a clearing out and as soon as the water went down the D. H. & I R.R. bridge was considered "shaky." Workmen were set to work at once placing stone around the piles to keep the water from doing them harm and trains were not delayed.

The loss of the dam was estimated at "not less than $2,000" and a drive was begun to raise the funds necessary for its reconstruction. This was apparently quickly done. The April 29 newspaper brought the news that construction had already begun.

The Raisin Floods Monroe

High water and ice in 1887 flooded both Front and Elm Street in downtown Monroe. Photographs taken that year show a steel bridge, with the planking washed away, and water halfway to the top of the arches. Miraculously both the inundated steel bridge and a wooden bridge upstream, survived the onslaught.

The high water caused two unusual accidents recorded in the *Monroe Record-Commercial*:

> While Frank Duvall and his 13-year-old son, Wilmer, were returning home on La Plaisance Road Thursday night from the residence of friends south of Otter Creek where they had been quietly celebrating the lad's 13th birthday, they drove across lower Otter Creek bridge and just after they got across the bridge and drawing down the grade which leads up to the bridge, the bottom of the grade being five or six feet below the surface of the bridge, the water in the hollow being about five feet deep and the current very swift they were suddenly swept from the road into the creek and their buggy overturned. The lad lost his hold of the buggy and was unable to get out of the rushing torrent. The father after a hard struggle and with the help of neighbors who heard his cries for help managed to reach the shore. The horse with the buggy swam ashore.

The body of the birthday boy was finally discovered on Sunday.

The same newspaper reports that Edward Beck, traveling on a plank road north of Monroe, reached a place in the road where the high water had washed out the planks. The horse fell in the opening, but Beck managed to cut the harness and free the animal as the buggy washed to the side of the road and lodged against a fence. He borrowed a buggy and managed to get home.

When Beck and a friend returned to get the buggy they found a man, his buggy, and his horse swept by the current up against a fence. The horse had drowned, but using fence boards they rescued the man.

The Highest Water in 1908

Photos of flooded buildings, taken near Monroe in 1908 show the river out

(Above) High water at Petersburg in 1908.

of its banks and up to the first floor window sills of houses built along the bank, But the worst flood in the Raisin valley, occurred in 1908 peaking at Blissfield on March 7, 1908, with the water level 30 ½ inches above flood stage. Seventy houses were surrounded by river waters, and there was 26 inches of water in the downtown stores.

3 Dams Fail at Manchester

At Manchester, which had three dams on the river, the ice and high water took out the upper structure on Valentine's Day, February 14, 1908, and began battering the foundry dam which succumbed on March 10. Shortly afterwards the third dam, which supplied electricity, washed out and the town went dark.

That very night, by torchlight, subscriptions were solicited to build a 10-foot temporary dam structure and the electric power and mill were back in business in a few days.

At Dundee on March 8, 1908, the river was so swollen, and the bridges either washed out or unusable, that a raft was used to transport a coffin across the rushing river to the other side for burial.

In May of 1914 there was rain and widespread flooding, but the peak was 12 inches lower than in 1908. One man at Dundee reported that he left his home to assist in efforts to stabilize the bridge and returned home to find his wife floating atop a kitchen table.

Last of the Old-Time Floods in 1947

The floods of 1947 are the last ones noted. That year a cold winter and thick ice which was late melting, met up with a steady rain which drove the rivers over their banks throughout lower Michigan.

Swollen rivers and creeks in Monroe County had started to return to normal today after a two-day rampage over the weekend. Countless acres of land were submerged when drains backed up and creeks turned into raging torrents. Roads were blocked in many directions, necessitating circuitous routes to those traveling. The River Raisin, Saline River and Huron River all reached their peaks yesterday and today were on the down grade... According to City Director Arthur Jennings, the strong west winds in conjunction with dry ground and little frost, resulted in the early and low peak. An east wind would have caused more serious trouble he said.[21]

Some disasters on the river had nothing to do with high water. A new iron bridge was erected over the River Raisin at Blissfield in 1875. On December 7, 1887, when the temperature was said to be 17 degrees below zero and the ice on the river was two feet thick. four men and seven cattle had just taken three steps on the bridge when, according to Charles Quigley, they "heard a great cracking and splitting all about them." The bridge dropped below them and crashed to the ice. Two men were injured. No one recorded what happened to the cattle.

Public opinion laid the blame for the collapse on the cast-iron cords beneath the bridge which had been tightened in preparation for the cold weather, when they should have been loosened instead. The people of Blissfield were forced to cross the river on the railroad bridge avoiding trains, and trying not to look down between the ties. In January of 1888, the citizens passed a bond issue for a new bridge by a vote of 258 to 12.

(Below) A bridge at Tecumseh. Ice added to the perils of spring floods.

240 Ft. Single Span Bridge, Second Largest Single Span Bridge in Michigan, Tecumseh, Mich.

Dams and Power Production

An 1893 assessment called the River Raisin "the most important milling stream of southeastern Michigan"[22] and listed 25 dams from Brooklyn to the mouth. About that time many dams were switching over to electric power generation and almost every community manufactured its own electricity until regional suppliers took over the task.

Electric Power Production

At Manchester J. H. Kingsley received a 10 year franchise from the village on February 10, 1892, "to do a general lighting business." He began operations in May of 1892 and eventually the business was sold out to Consumers Power in 1926.

In Blissfield the old dam north of town was expanded by a power plant built in June of 1899 and production began. It was enlarged in 1910 and again in 1920, assisted by a new steel and concrete dam built with the encouragement of the local sugar beet company and the village council in 1912. The operation was sold to Consumers Power in 1950.

In Dundee the first dam was built of brush in 1827, rebuilt with logs in 1846, with old railroad ties in 1897 and concrete in 1909. It powered the Dundee Hydraulic Power Company's operation until 1910 when the operation was bought out by Detroit Edison Company, the southernmost in the company's area.

The tiny community of Grape in Monroe County, between Dundee and Monroe, was known for its lime kilns. For several years a small hydroelectric plant produced what the local people used to call "grape juice."

Power house at Tecumseh about 1909

Ford's Village Industries Experiment

In 1922, automotive innovator and manufacturer Henry Ford wrote:

> Every social ailment from which we suffer today originates and centers in the great cities. But

you will find the smaller communities living along in unison with the seasons, having neither extreme poverty nor wealth, and none of the violent plagues of upheaval and unrest which afflict our great populations.[23]

Ford was a great advocate of "water power" which he called "the cheapest, the most efficient, and the least wasteful of all types of power."[24]

Combining the two passions in 1920 he began to experiment with moving selected portions of automotive manufacturing away from the central factory and out into the small towns within about 50 miles of the Ford headquarters at Dearborn. For the most part the plan was to utilize defunct mills and already-constructed dams and races.

First Plants on Rouge River

The first of the "village industries" was begun in 1920 at Northville on the River Rouge, when an old sawmill was renovated to produce valves for automobiles. This was followed quickly by Nankin Mills, Phoenix and Plymouth on the River Rouge and Flat Rock on the Huron River.

With the beginning of the depression the program, which offered jobs to rural workers, was seen as an effort to bolster the economy of the small towns and spread the shrinking number of paychecks around. In 1932 a plant was opened in Ypsilanti on the Huron and in 1935 in Newburgh on the Rouge. Then Henry's eye turned to the nearby River Raisin.

River Raisin Works for Ford

In 1935 he opened a factory in a restored 1898 flour mill in Tecumseh known as Hayden Mills. There a small work force was set to work cleaning, sacking and storing soybeans grown nearby and used in the manufacture of plastic parts for cars. The following year Ford opened a village industry in the old grist mill at Dundee. There as many as 125 workers manufactured copper welding tips.

As war loomed additional small factories were added to the program. In 1939, a new building on the site of an old gristmill at Brooklyn was used to make

The old dam site at Brooklyn with the new plant Ford built in 1939.

(Above) Sharon Mills, used by Ford 1939 to 1947 has been restored and is now part of the Washtenaw County parks system and is open for tours. The machinery is on display behind windows, even when the building is closed. (Below) Hayden Mills at Tecumseh from a 1940s postcard. The plant was used by Ford from 1935 to 1948.

Ford vehicle horn buttons and starter switches, later changing to plastic lamp lenses and armrests. The same year a plant opened in an 1835 gristmill at Sharonville for the manufacture of cigar lighters (Ford did not approve of cigarette smoking), electrical switches and generator ammeters.

In 1941 the last of the Raisin River sites opened in a new building on the site of an old gristmill at Manchester. There up to 279 workers built ammeters for instrument clusters.

Factory and Farm

Part of the original plan included work on the farm during slow times at the factory. As Ford expressed it, "One foot in industry and one foot in the soil." Also, each worker was allotted a small plot of land where he was expected to grow food for his family (during World War II such areas were known as victory gardens).

The facilities themselves were model plants, most with generators displayed in glass enclosures so that visitors could stand outside of the plant and watch the hydroelectric power at work. The factories were also landscaped and looked like old-fashioned buildings in a park setting. The Sharon Mills operation has been restored to its Ford-era appearance and is administered by the Washtenaw County Park system.

After World War II these small plants were phased out of production, but only gradually. On the Raisin the cigar lighter plant at Sharon Mills closed in 1947; the Hayden Mill at Tecumseh closed in 1948; the plant at Dundee closed in 1954 but the facilities were in use by the Wolverine Fabricating and Manufacturing Company until 1970. Ford left Manchester in 1957, but several companies used the facilities into the 1990s. The Brooklyn operation closed in 1967, but the facilities were in use until the 1980s by Industrial Automotive Products, a subsidiary of Jackson Gear.

Big Time Power Production

In 1905 the Detroit Edison Company, which supplied power for most of the Detroit area, attempted to purchase the Monroe municipal electric plant, but was turned down by the voters. It was not until 1917 that Detroit Edison Company acquired the facilities and territory, the southernmost of its service area.

In 1953 Detroit Edison purchased 1,200 acres of land along the River Raisin between the city and Lake Erie. They bought land on the river with no thought of using hydropower to produce electricity, but rather to have an alternate way to ship coal to the plant. A later history noted that the possibility of water transportation "would aid in price negotiation with the railroad, even though the railroad was from the first the designated agent."[25]

The property included the old bed of the River Raisin as it headed to its earlier mouth on La Plaisance Bay. Before approval for the erection of a power plant at that site Congress passed, and President Lyndon B. Johnson signed, an Omnibus Bill which included the declaration that the old channel of the River Raisin was no longer a navigable stream. This action cleared the way for incorporation of the old bed into plans for the new plant.

Construction began in 1966 and the plans grew as the project developed until four nearly identical units, utilizing two large smokestacks, sat on the south bank of the mouth of the River Raisin, producing more than 3,200,000 kilowatts. In 2000 the Monroe plant had the third largest generating capacity of any coal-fired plant in North America behind only the Southern Company's Plant Bowen located near Atlanta, and Ontario Power Generation's Nanticoke Generating Station in Canada.

In January of 1996 Detroit Edison became part of a new holding company called DTE Energy, which is now the owner-of-record for the Monroe facility. President George W. Bush toured the plan in September of 2003 to view modernization efforts, and give an address on power production and homeland security.

However as the price of land transportation increased the power plant began doing what it had earlier stated it would not do – receive the delivery of coal by water.

Even as an average of three long trains a day continue to bring in coal by rail, during the navigational season several bulk carriers each month put into the DTE docks near the mouth of the river with coal deliveries.

Although Edison has permitted the establishment of fishing docks near the plant on the south bank of the river, swimmers can no longer access the beach on either side. Most of the land around the mouth of the river is devoted to heavy industry.

(Below) Industry at the mouth of the river, based on a 2004 navigational chart.

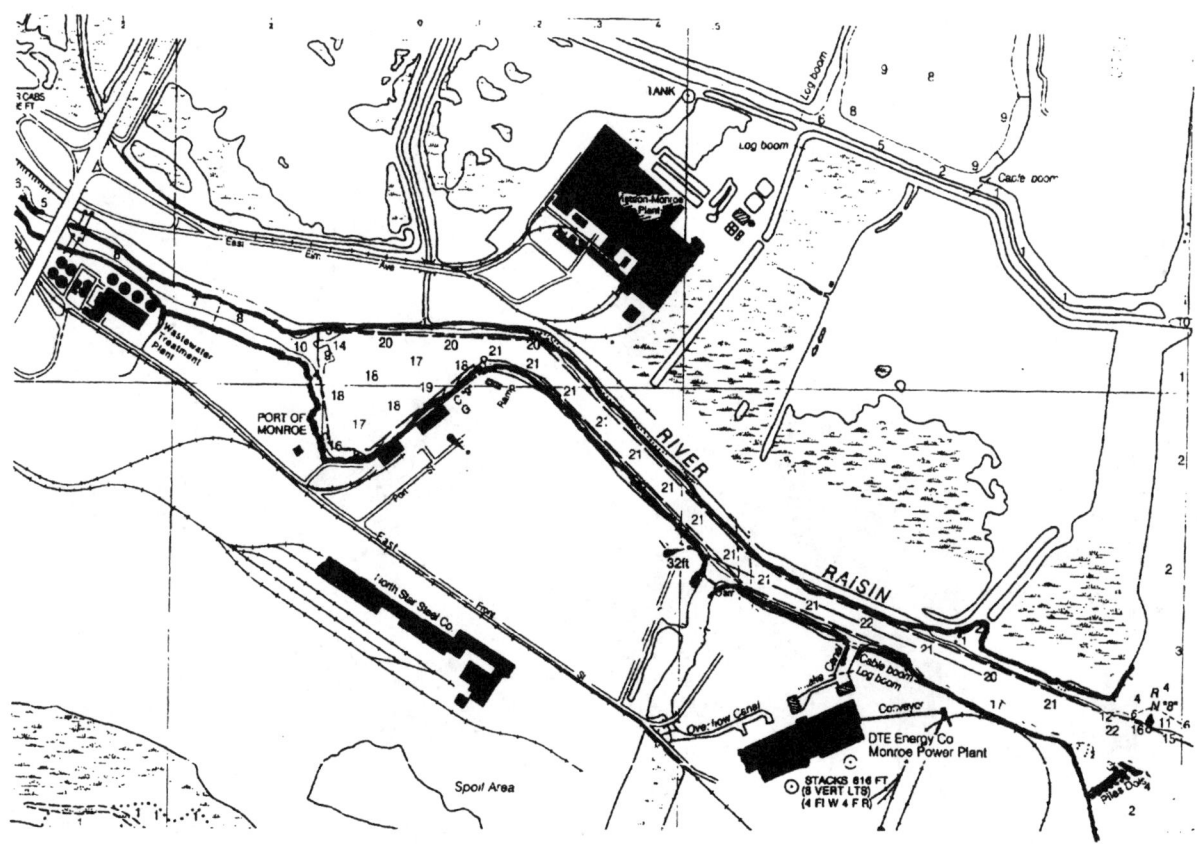

Monroe Piers, Monroe, Mich.

Two postcards from 1909 show the height of popularity of Monroe's piers with day trippers and resorters. The building at right in both pictures is the Monroe Yacht Club. (Above) five sailboats make their way out onto Lake Erie, past the casino and changing rooms, and a refreshment stand. At far right the top of the lighthouse is seen behind the boat club. (Below) a well-dressed couple strolls on the boardwalk at the beach end of the north pier.

Ecological Future

From the late 1800s to the mid-1920s, in the summertime at least, Monroe, and most especially the river mouth, was the center of good times.

Summertime at the Piers

In 1910 the vacationer or day visitor from Detroit or Toledo could ride the interurban directly to the pier heads where the young people could stroll along the north pier out to the lighthouse and visit the keeper's residence. The kids might go for a ride on the merry-go-round. Rowing clubs set up races and the Monroe Yacht Club, founded in 1886, organized sailing outings, regattas, and muskrat dinners. There was a nearby refreshment stand for more conventional fare and a changing house which could accommodate more than 300 swimmers, renting, for 25 cents, a bathing suit, a towel and a locker with a key.

Focal point of the complex was the casino, which operated almost year-round, on the piers themselves, with a nearby saloon. There was also the Hotel Lotus, on the Lake Erie beach, and acres of floating lotus plants, sometimes called water lilies. A popular boat trip in the summer took visitors right into the lotus beds where they could view, photograph and gather the blossoms.

The Beginning of the End

World War I first put a crimp in the summertime attendance. A terrible interurban collision, which killed 11 and injured 27, only enhanced the growing popularity of the automobile and the many alternative activities it offered.

In 1927 the Hotel Lotus was demolished to clear the beach area for industrial production, chiefly a new plant by the Newton Steel Company. The following year the Detroit, Monroe & Toledo Shoreline electric train halted service. In 1922 the lighthouse, which had been replaced by an automated gas light, was sold, dismantled and carried away. Several years later the casino was moved to Sterling State Park which was established in 1936 along the Lake Erie shore to the north. (The building was torn down in the late 1940s.) The yacht club attempted to float its building across Brest Bay, but it sank.

Water Quality Questioned in 1873

How much water quality figured into this metamorphosis from frivolity to heavy industry is not clear, but contemporary resources describe a river and a lake where if people were not concerned, they should have been.

As early as 1873 the City of Adrian was attempting to create an elevated reservoir for fire protection and the proposal called for getting the water from Wolf Creek, near its intersection with the River Raisin. The city fathers objected "because the River Raisin was contaminated with sewage." [26]

It was not until 1923 that Adrian was forced by the state to build a sewage system. The full system was voted down, but a scaled-down project at least

> **FISH CONSUMPTION ADVISORY**
>
> **Certain kinds and sizes of fish contain levels of toxic chemicals that may be harmful if those fish are eaten too often.**
>
> The amounts of chemicals found in Michigan fish are not known to cause immediate sickness. But chemicals can collect in the body over time. It may take months or years of regularly eating contaminated fish to build up amounts that are a health concern. Chemicals may eventually affect your health or that of your children.
>
> **RIVER RAISIN**
>
> **Above Monroe Dam:**
>
> General Population: unlimited consumption of Carp
>
> Women & Children: Carp, one meal per month.
>
> **Downstream from Monroe Dam:**
>
> General Population: Do not eat these fish: Black Buffalo over 14 inches, Carp, Channel Catfish, White Bass over 12 inches; one meal a week, Smallmouth bass over 14 inches, White Bass 10 to 12 inches; unlimited consumption, Black Buffalo under 14 inches, Freshwater Drum, White Bass under 10 inches.
>
> Women & Children: Do not eat these fish: Black Buffalo over 14 inches, Carp, Channel Catfish, White Bass over 12 inches; one meal a month, Freshwater Drum; six meals per year, Black Buffalo under 14 inches, Smallmouth Bass, White Bass under 12 inches.

A summary of the State of Michigan Fish Consumption Advisory issued in 2007. All the fish for which it recommends limiting consumption are suspected of harboring PCB contamination.

halted the practice of dumping the raw sewage directly into the river.

In 1951 the Village of Blissfield was ordered to built a sewage treatment facility. Ground was broken in April of 1956; by April, 1981, the area needed a new plant.

Raisin "Hard to keep safe."

During the Blissfield construction the Michigan Water Resources Commission admitted aloud, "River Raisin is one of the most difficult sources of water in Michigan to treat and keep safe."

The River Raisin, which for many years had large paper mills upstream and other pollution-creating plants empties into Lake Erie which, in the 1960s was being called a "dead lake" as high phosphorous levels led to an increase of algae which befouled the shores and contributed to massive fish kills.

In 1969 when the Cuyahoga River at Cleveland, Ohio, on its way to Lake Erie, became so polluted with petrochemicals that it actually caught fire, embarrassed state and local officials decided that something had to be done, resulting, among other things, in the Clean Water Act of 1972.

An "Area of Concern"

The final 2.65 miles of the Raisin out into Lake Erie was declared an "Area of Concern," where pollution called for immediate measures. Clean-up began with a cease and desist order issued by the Michigan Department of Natural Resources in 1975, to stop the dumping of wastes into the low land near the mouth of the Raisin.

Traditionally low, boggy areas, good for nothing else, were tapped as places to dump waste. The swamps around the mouth of the River Raisin for many years were an active dumping ground for all kinds of industrial by-products.

A work of remediation was begun to deal with the wastes already dumped there, 1940 to 1975. In 1983 a permanent dike was constructed from I-75 east to the McMillan canal which discharges hot water from the Edison power plant. A two and a half foot slurry wall runs along the entire 7,300 feet of the dike extending to a depth of 20 feet. This construction is designed to stop the filling of Plum Creek Bay and to contain the Port of Monroe landfill.

Plating wastes which had been deposited in the wetlands next to Sterling State Park are contained in new modern facilities. A dike protects the Plum Creek Wildlife Area from further contamination.[27]

The PCB Problem

Another serious problem, for which a plan-of-action is ongoing is PCBs (Polychlorinated Biphenyls). This chemical compound is a mixture of oil-based chemicals widely used as a fire retardant in electrical equipment. It was banned in 1979 by the U.S. Environmental Protection Agency.

Testing on animals indicates that PCBs probably cause cancer and other illness. The chemical adheres to solids and settles into the river sediment, then accumulates in the fatty tissue of aquatic organisms and can be transmitted through the food chain.[28]

Small Mouth Bass (top) and Walleye were two game fish discovered in the Raisin River during a 1984 survey.

Sampling the Fish Population

A 1984 survey of fish which sampled fishing at 12 sites along the River Raisin caught over 85,000 fish representing 61 species, including Bluenose Minnow, Northern Hog Sucker, but also "populations of Smallmouth Bass, Northern Pike and Rock Bass were available to offer moderate fishing opportunities at several locations. . . in addition Walleye, Yellow Perch, Bluegill, Sunfish, and Largemouth Bass were found."[29]

The 1984 study showed a trend to better fishing, "In comparison with a survey in 1971, conditions for sport fishing improved below Dundee, owing to a reduction in pollution from populated areas. In 1971 fish populations were low even in areas with good stream bottoms of gravel, etc. In 1984 poor fish areas were "where the bottom was poor and the water was muddy."[30] The report recommended continuing efforts at improving water quality, especially limiting sediment caused by poor agricultural practices, and that the stocking of sport fish be studied.

Citizens Get Busy

A number of organizations have been created to focus on the problems and discuss solutions.

The River Raisin Watershed Council was formed in 1974 to provide a place where all of the communities in the watershed could unite behind its mission to protect and preserve the watershed. Also "to inspire behaviors that enhance and sustain the River Raisin through advocacy, classroom and public education, water quality, monitoring, volunteer clear-ups and encourage recreation on the river."[31]

The Raisin Valley Land Trust was formed "to preserve natural areas, historical structures, active farmland and scenic roads" and "to promote public awareness of these natural features and actively engage individuals and communities to help preserve them"[32] The Trust encourages conservation easements and/or the donation of land to the trust.

The University of Toledo, through its Lake Erie Center, is dedicated to solving environmental problems at the land-water interface. The research and teaching facility is located in the northwest corner of Ohio's Maumee Bay State Park.

Post-Remediation Sampling

In 2002 the Great Lakes National Program Office, in conjunction with the U. S. Army Corps of Engineers of the Detroit District and the Michigan Department of Environmental Quality conducted an extensive survey of sediment quality conditions within the River Raisin Area of Concern,

The main focus of the study was to evaluate the levels of PCB remaining following a sediment removal project completed in 1997 with the cooperation of the Ford Stamping Plant.

The results of the survey demonstrated that PCB contamination was still "a significant problem within the Area of Concern, from the sediment removal project, downstream to the mouth of the river."[33]

The report stated that the sediment testing and the analysis of caged fish in the area indicated that there was still "the potential for contaminant uptake into the food web, and suggest that PCBs remaining in the sediment removal area and in downstream areas may continued to present a human health and ecological risk."[34]

The report recommended examining several sources for the continued contamination including the sloughing of contaminated sediments from the adjacent navigational channel, and residual contamination from the completed dredging project.

(Above) Lotus blossoms in the marshland between downtown Monroe and Lake Erie about 1910.

The 2007 Fish Consumption Advisory issued by the State of Michigan recommends that diners limit their fish consumption, especially for certain species for fish caught below the Monroe dam, and in the area of the river mouth in Lake Erie. (See page 44 for a summary the 2007 Fish Consumption Advisory.)

Lotus Blossoms Return

The American Lotus (*Nelumbo hitea*), a large aquatic wildflower, which was once so abundant in the wetlands surrounding the river's mouth, began to disappear with the industrialization of the harbor and the contamination from the factories which filled the shallow waters.

The acres of plants that the Indians had tapped for food, eating the nut-like seeds as well as boiling the roots like potatoes, disappeared, and only an occasional plant was found in secluded areas.[35]

But some area people tried hard to assist the plants, harvesting the abundant seeds of the few plants left, covering the seeds with a mud ball and returning them to the marshy areas.

Today lowered water levels and clean-up efforts have also led to the reemergence of the lotus flowers. Visitors come from all over the world to view, but no longer to pick, the flowers during the mid-summer blooming season.

The official symbol for clean water in the State of Michigan is the American Lotus. The City of Monroe also sports a stylized lotus on its seal, and the motif is seen on park buildings.

Recreational boating near the mouth of the river is well-served by the Hellenberg Boat Launch and other new and established facilities. The Monroe Boat Club, successor to the old Monroe Yacht Club and Bolles Harbor Boat Club continue summer events.

Making Progress

Costs of restoring the River Raisin and the nearby areas of Lake Erie reached the $40 million mark in 2007 and the work continues. The River Raisin and Lake Erie are improving in water quality and recreational possibilities, but there is still a long way to go.

The River Raisin Watershed Council wants to move onward. "Remediation has taken the place of reclamation," the council declares, but it also has a new project:

> What remains to be done? Monroe Harbor is on the St. Lawrence Seaway. If the Harbor is brought to Seaway depth, 28 feet, the resulting modification will result in the restoration of Raisin Point and the Monroe Marshes, which will be reclaimed from the shallows of LaPlaisance Bay. In 1980, the U. S. Army Corps of Engineers proposed to build a Confined Disposal Facility on Raisin Point. The structure would provide a wave shadow zone for Bolles Harbor to protect the recreational navigation channel and harbor of refuge. Nearly 800 acres of wetland would be created behind the barrier restoring the River Raisin estuary to its former glory.[36]

Sourcenotes

[1] Blois, John T. *Gazetteer of the State of Michigan* (Sydney L. Rood & Co.: Detroit) 1838, p. 349.

[2] Larson, John W. *Essayons: A History of the Detroit District U. S. Army Corps of Engineers* (U.S. Army Corps of Engineers, Detroit District) 1981, p. 33.

[3] Joseph Bradish to John Bradish, February 7, 1819. Bentley Historical Library, University of Michigan, Ann Arbor.

[4] *History of the Great Lakes, Illustrated* (J.J. Beers & Co.: Chicago) 1881, p.308.

[5] Hatcher, Harlan *Lake Erie* (Bobbs-Merrill Company: Indianapolis) 1945, p. 34.

[6] Elizabeth Margaret Chandler to Jane Howard, June 15, 1831, Elizabeth Margaret Chandler Collection, Bentley Historical Library, University of Michigan, Ann Arbor.

[7] Bonner, Richard Illenden, ed. *Memoirs of Lenawee County, Michigan* (Western Historical Association: Madison, Wisconsin) 1909, p. 25.

[8] Bonner, op.cit., p. 19-20.

[9] Hinsdale, Wilbert B. *Archeological Atlas of Michigan* (University of Michigan Press: Ann Arbor) 1931.

[10] Ellis, Edward D., *Michigan Sentinel*, January 10, 1829. (Editorial)

[11] Clark, Thomas. Address to the Pioneer Society of Lenawee County, June 10, 1878. *MPHC II*, p. 423-424.

[12] Wing, Talcott E. "History of Monroe County, Michigan," *MPHC IV*, p. 320.

[13] Dudley, Thomas P. "Battle and Massacre at Frenchtown, Michigan, January, 1813," *MPHC, XX*, p. 437,

[14] Wing, *op cit*, p. 322.

[15] Statement dated Lexington KY, May 2, 1813. American State Papers, Military Affairs, I, p. 372-373.

[16] Squire Reynolds quoted in Coffin, William F. *1812: The War, and its Moral: A Canadian Chronicle* (John Lovell : Montreal) 1864, p. 206.

[17] Young, Bennett H. *The Battle of the Thames* (John P. Morton and Company: Louisville, Kentucky) 1903, p. 76-77.

[18] *The Record-Commercial*, September 8, 1904.

[19] *History of Washtenaw County, Michigan* (Chas. C. Chapman & Co.: Chicago) 1881, p. 581-582.

[20] *ibid.* p. 1296

[21] *Monroe Evening News*, April 7, 1947

[22] *Michigan and Its Resources* (Robert Smith & Co., State Printers: Lansing) 1893, p. 93.

[23] Miller, James Martin *The Amazing Story of Henry Ford* (James C. Bailey & Company: Chicago) 1922, Ch. 23.

[24] Segal, Howard P. *Recasting the Machine Age: Henry Ford's Village Industries* (University of Massachusetts Press: Amherst) 2005.

[25] Miller, Raymond C. *The Force of Energy: A Business History of the Detroit Edison Company* (Michigan State University Press) 1971, p.219

[26] Linquist, Charles *Adrian; The City That Worked* (Lenawee County Historical Society: Adrian) 2004, p. 63.

[27] "History of the River Raisin," The River Raisin Watershed Council. Retrieved 8/31/2008 from http://riverraisin.org.

[28] *River Raisin Watershed Map*, The River Raisin Watershed Council, n.d.

[29] Towns, Gary L. *A Fisheries Survey of the River Raisin* (Fisheries Division, Michigan Department of Natural Resources: Lansing) 1985.

[30] *ibid.*

[31] U. S. Environmental Protection Agency, "Adopt Your Watershed." Retrieved 8/25/2008 from http://yosemite.epa.gov/water/adopt.nsf/

[32] *ibid*

[33] "Post-Remediation Sediment Sampling on the Raisin River Near Monroe, Michigan" (U. S. Environmental Protection Agency) 2002.

[34] *ibid.*

[35] Place, Ruth Mosher, "Thirty Michigan Wildflowers," *Wildflowers of Michigan* (Michigan Department of Conservation and Federated Garden Clubs of Michigan) 1940?

[36] River Raisin Watershed Council, "History of the River Raisin." Retrieved 8/31/2008 from http://riverraisin.org/about/history.html

From Beginning to End

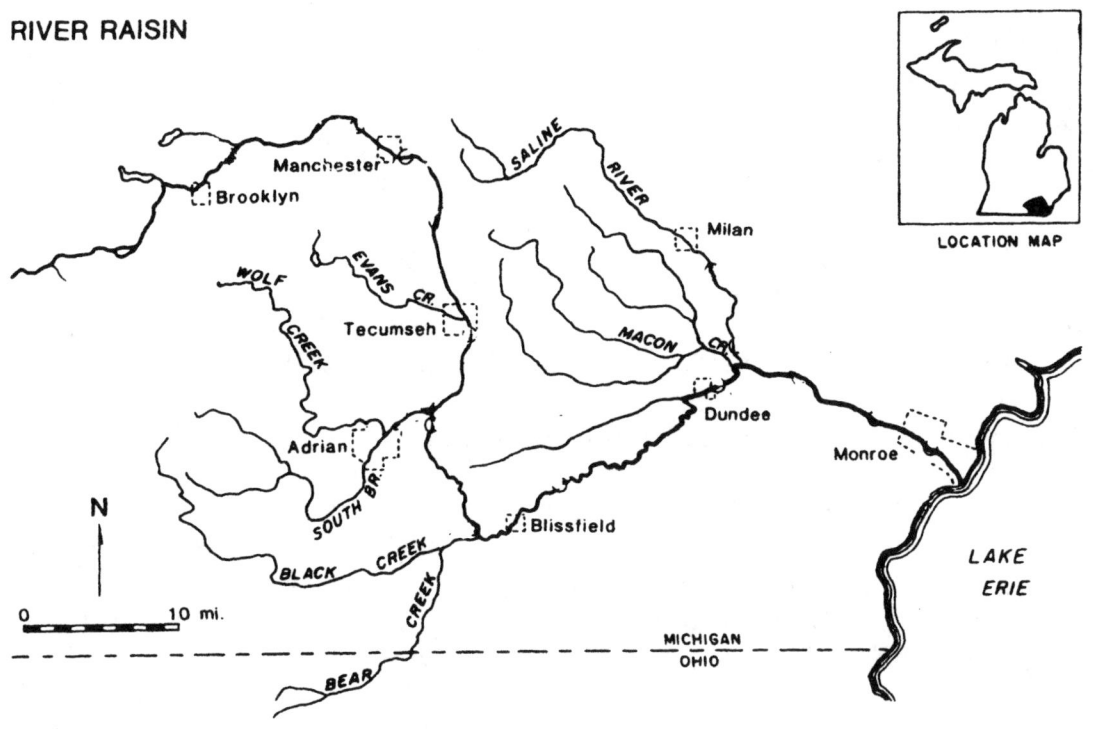

This tour of the River Raisin is based on U. S. Geological Survey topographical maps from 1909 to 1980. It is a mile-by-mile account, as measured on the most recent version of the maps, of what you would see if you were paddling a canoe down the river, despite the fact that such a trip would be impossible over some of the river's length because of shallow water, downed trees, weed-choked channels, culverts, bridges, dams and other manmade improvements. Maps, both old and new, and many historic photographs show the changing face of the river.

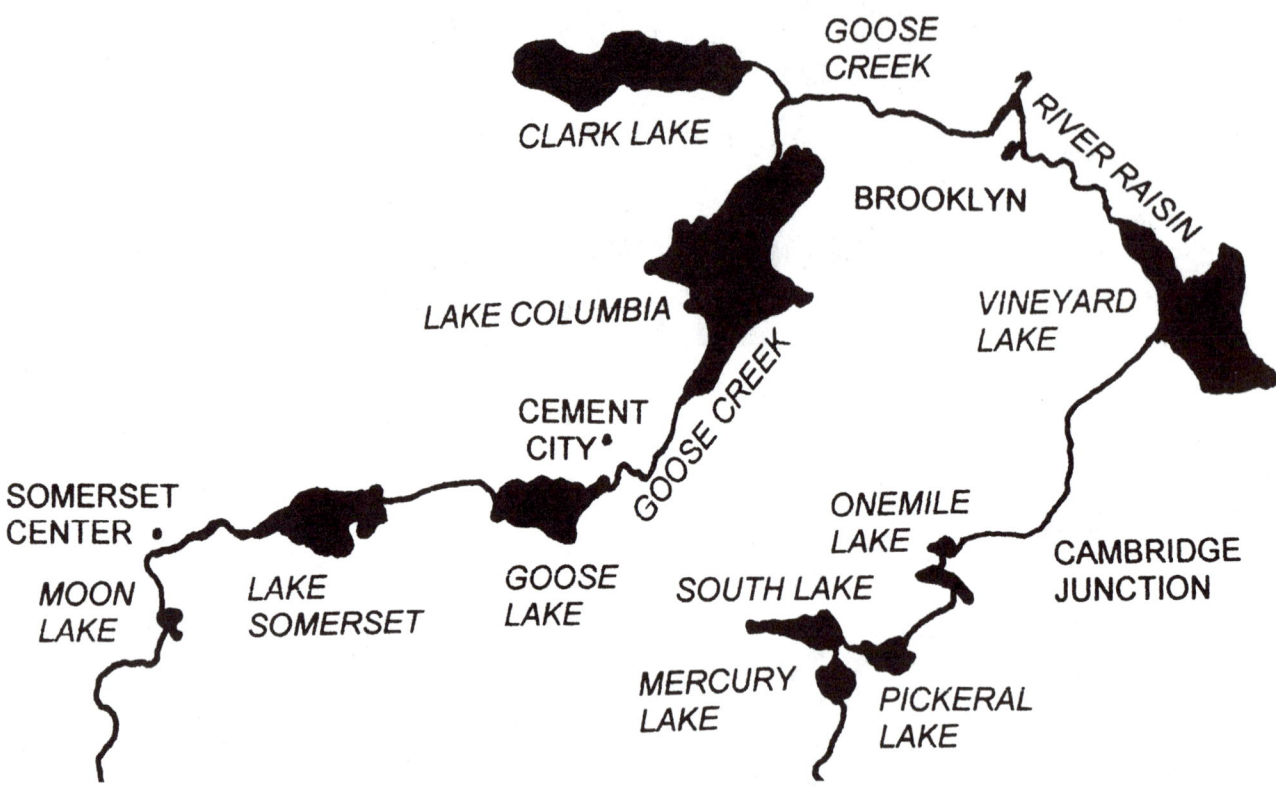

The River Raisin, like most rivers, changes in length and direction as the river bed changes over time, and follows a slightly different path at different water levels.

A description in an 1881 history of Jackson County notes:

> The Raisin river may be said to have its origin in Norvill township where its main feeder flows from the millpond and thus is it made a continuation of Goose Creek, the source of which is found in Columbia, the adjoining township. The second feeder rises in Grass lake, and flowing south, forms a junction with the main branch, south of Sweeney *[probably Swezzey]* Lake. . .

Most maps, contemporary and historic, show the main stream beginning in a series of lakes southwest of Brooklyn. The Grass Lake connection disappeared during the drainage of farmland and development although remnants of the old stream may be seen in Sharonville State Wildlife Management Area, and in a small stream which joins the river between Mud and Swezzey Lakes at mile 117.5.

The Goose Creek connection continues. This stream should be considered one of the Raisin's primary sources. It is the most westerly part of the Raisin watershed and represents the highest elevation, it being in Michigan's Irish Hills. The area is a birthing place for rivers. Three rivers head off to Lake Michigan: the Grand which terminates at Grand Haven, the Kalamazoo which enters the big lake at Saugatuck and the St. Joseph which travels south to Indiana then enters Lake Michigan at Benton Harbor-St. Joseph. In the same area the St. Joseph River of the Maumee begins its journey to Lake Erie at Toledo and the River Raisin flows to Monroe. The five rivers all rise within a few miles of each other, sometimes with only a half mile separating the main streams.

Sources: The Goose Creek Connection

Miles in this section represent the number of miles to the junction of Goose Creek with the River Raisin just north of Brooklyn at main river mile 122.95. It is sometimes hard to pinpoint exact sources in a swamp. This appeared to be the start of the creek in the summer of 2008; with less precipitation details may vary.

15.5. Goose Creek rises near the east edge of section 28, Somerset Township, Hillsdale County, three miles south and slightly west of the community of Somerset Center. It begins in a swamp, surrounded by higher land from 1050 to 1060 feet in elevation, just south of Mercer Road, and west of Waldron Road.

15.4 Culvert. Mercer Road crosses east-west.

14.4 Culvert. Sand Hill Road crosses east-west.

13.4 Culvert. Waldron Road crosses the flow north-south.

12.8-12.6 Enter Moon Lake on the south-center, and exit on the northwest.

12.2 Site of old railroad crossing.

12 - 11.4 **Somerset Center** began in 1833 when Elias Alley built the first residence. It was named because it was near the center of Somerset Township, which had been named for Somerset, Niagara County, New York. A post office was established in this area about 1835, first named **Gambleville**. The office was moved back and forth from Somerset to Somerset Center until it closed in 1893. The settlement was located on the old territorial road to Chicago. Less than half a mile to the

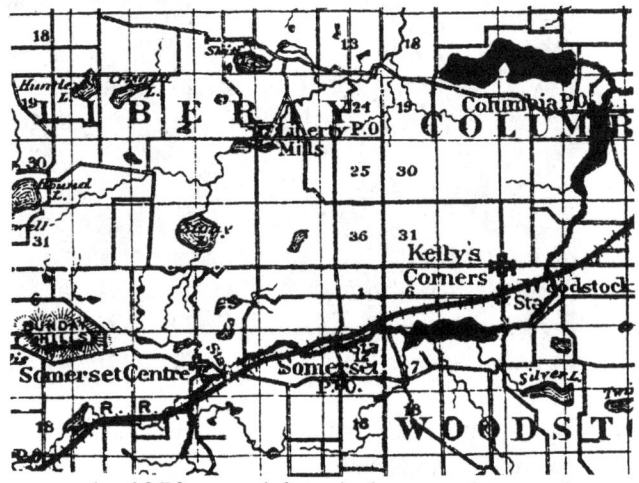

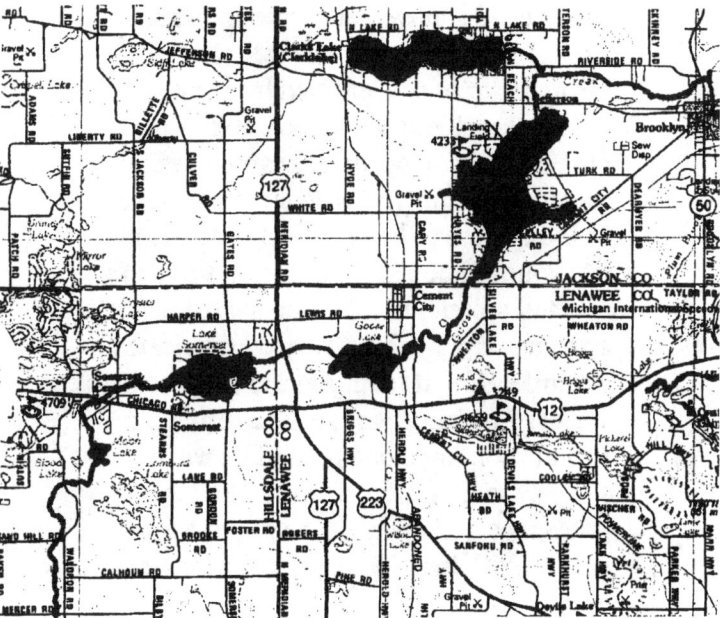

An 1873 map (above) shows only a wide spot where Lake Columbia would later be, and no sign at all of Lake Somerset. Kelly's Corners would become Cement City, Columbia would change its name to Jefferson. Somerset Center is on the left on both maps, the lower one based on a 2006 survey.

(Above) A cement bridge in McCourtie Park.

west lies Lake LeAnn, a primary source of the Grand River.

11.8 Bridge. Chicago Road, U. S. 12, crosses the creek east-west in downtown Somerset Center. The bridge has guardrails and some stonework.

11.7 – 5 **McCourtie Park**. The former estate of cement magnate W. H. L. McCourtie is now a Somerset Township Park. The small stream as it flows through the park is crossed by eight bridges, each one a different style, created by Mexico artisans about 1930 in the *Trabajo Rustico* style, cement shaped to look like tree limbs. Outside of the old McCourtie house near the road, there are two tall splintered tree trunks, also of cement, which are actually chimneys for an underground room, said to have been visited by Henry Ford, and, during Prohibition, by members of Detroit's Purple Gang. Each bridge is fitted to the landscape and many of the rocks, designed to look like part of the stream, are also handcrafted.

11.4 Bridge. South Jackson Road crosses Goose Creek north-south.

10.8 - 9.4 The flow enters Lake Somerset, elevation 1022 feet, on the west. The lake is approximately 188 acres. The settlement of **Somerset** is located near the southeast shore of the lake on the old highway. Somerset Lake is entirely in private hands, administered by the Lake Somerset Property Owners Association.

9.4 Earthen Dam with an overflow apparatus in the lake. Water exits out the northeast corner of Lake Somerset. The dam is 29.7 feet in height.

8.95 Enter Woodstock Township, Lenawee County, crossing the prime meridian for the State of Michigan.

8.85 Bridge. U. S. 127 crosses north-south

8-7.1 Enter Goose Lake on the northwest shore and exit from the east. The village of **Cement City** touches the northeast end of Goose Lake. From 1838 to about 1886, operating sporadically at times, it was the site of the early post office of **Woodstock**, named for the township which had been named for Woodstock, Vermont. The post office was renamed **Cement** and then Cement City in 1901, to mark the coming of a cement company. Incorporated as a village in 1953.

7. Railroad Bridge. Channel between Goose Lake and Little Goose Lake is crossed by a railroad bridge.

7. - 6.8 Little Goose Lake. The creek enters Little Goose Lake at the southwest corner and exits about halfway up the eastern shore, then turns north into a long swampy area.

6.8 Bridge. Cary Road crosses the creek north-south.

5.5 Bridge Taylor Road (called Vicary Road in Jackson County) which runs along the county line crosses the creek east-west.

5.5 Enter Columbia Township, Jackson County.

5.5 - 3 Enter Lake Columbia at the southernmost point and exit slightly northwest of center near the community of Jefferson. The elevation of Lake Columbia is 988 feet. The lake is nearly 800 acres in area.

3. Dam. On an 1870s map there is a wide spot in the river here labeled "Mill Pond." Since then the dam has been increased to 33 feet creating a much enlarged body of water now called Lake Columbia.

(Below) Lake Somerset from the top of the earthen dam.

Jefferson, on the north shore of Columbia Lake, just north of the dam, was settled in 1834 by Anson H. DeLamatter, and platted the following year. It was given a post office named **Columbia** after the township June 27, 1839, with DeWitt C. DeLamatter as postmaster. The post office operated until 1875. The community was named for President Thomas Jefferson.

2.7 Bridge. Jefferson road crosses Goose Creek east-west.

2.3 The outlet from Clark Lake enters Goose Creek from the northwest. Clark Lake is over a mile in length, and a half a mile wide over most of its length. Its eastern edge is only about a half mile east of the main channel of the Grand River as it begins its journey to Lake Michigan.

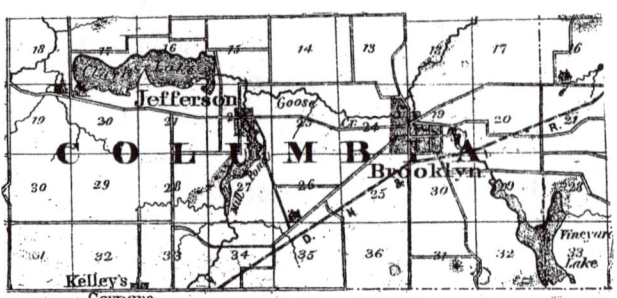

This map from an 1879 Hillsdale County atlas shows a dam on Goose Creek at Jefferson creating a mill pond.

.15 Bridge. Brooklyn Road, M-50, crosses the creek north-south.

0 Junction with the main stream of the River Raisin at mile 122.95 of the main river.

(Below) A 1941 postcard view of Clark Lake.

Sources: Main River

Numbers in this section represent the number of miles to Lake Erie via the main channel of the River Raisin and the Monroe Canal.

133 The main stream of the River Raisin rises in section 26 of Woodstock Township, Lenawee County, in a swampy area just west of Round Lake Road. Elevations around the low area are 1040 to 1046 feet. The stream flows northeasterly through the swamp.

132.5 Culvert. Round Lake Highway crosses north-south.

132.1 Culvert. The water flows west under Round Lake Highway.

131.8 Flow enters Mercury Lake on the southeast corner.

131.5 Culvert. Cooley Road crosses the middle of Mercury Lake east-west.

131.4 Flow exits Mercury Lake and flows through a channel to South Lake, entering the larger lake at the southeastern end. The elevation at South Lake is 998 feet.

131.2 The creek exits South Lake and flows eastward to Pickerel Lake.

131.15 Culvert. Round Lake Road crosses the creek north-south as it goes between South and Pickerel Lakes..

130.9-130.5 The flow enters Pickerel Lake, leaving from the northeastern corner.

129.9-129.75 The water flows into Onemile Lake, elevation 985 feet, on the southwestern side of the lake, and exits on the northwest. Several of the smaller lakes to the north may receive part of the flow at some water levels. Onemile Lake, Cleveland Lake and several smaller bodies of water are all part of the Onsted State Wildlife Management Area. In periods of low water, there is

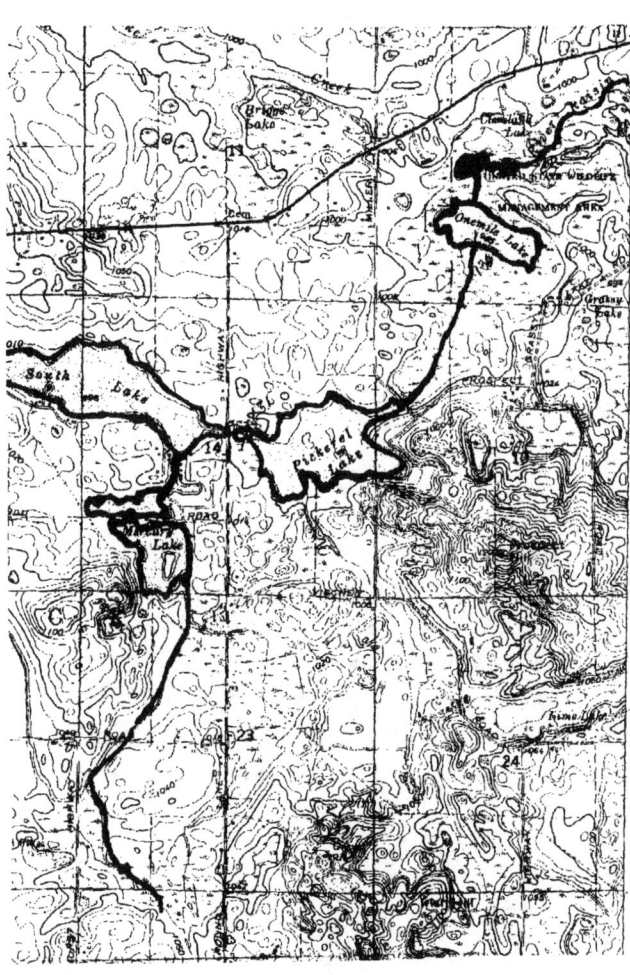

At normal water levels the River Raisin rises in section 26 of Woodstock Township and passes through a number of small lakes before heading off to the northeast toward Brooklyn.

little flow from the southern lakes and the river might be said to rise here.

129 Enter Cambridge Township, Lenawee County

128.4 Bridge. U. S. 12 crosses east-west. **Cambridge Junction Historic Park** is a mile to the east. Also known as the Walker Tavern Complex, two of the earliest roads in Michigan crossed at this point and Sylvester Walker by 1840 ran a tavern there. The tavern, constructed about 1836, a barn, 66 acres of rolling ground, and a visitor center, housed in a southern mansion-style home built by a later owner, is administered as a Michigan State Park with an on-site historian. A second tavern, built at this crossing in the early 1850s, is located across the road and is not part of the park.

128.4 Culvert. Triple culvert crosses the river east-west. The small stream flows down the east side of the Michigan International Speedway complex and is crossed by a small access road which is also used in the fall for the high school cross-country state meet.

127.7 Culvert. Still on the Speedway grounds an unpaved road crosses the river east-west, as the east bank gets steeper.

127.4 Enter Columbia Township, Jackson County.

127.2 Bridge. M-50 crosses southeast to northwest

127.05 The outlet from Phelps Lake enters the river from the south. This stream may be considered a third primary source. It begins about a mile southwest of Cambridge Junction at Little Stony Lake, elevation 991 feet. The stream flows through several smaller bodies of water and around Cambridge Junction before becoming the outlet for Phelps Lake and joining the River Raisin just northeast of the Speedway.

127 Bridge. Monroe Pike Road crosses the river north-south.

126.4 Bridge. Ventura Road crosses the river east-west.

The view from the northern culvert on the International Speedway grounds.

Little has changed at Cambridge Junction over the last 150 years except that the two roads that form the junction at that point keep getting wider and faster. The postcard above was taken in the early 1940s, showing the brick tavern at left, and the smaller, older wooden structure across the street. In the 2007 photo below the brick tavern is for sale, and the older building is part of a Michigan State Historic Park.

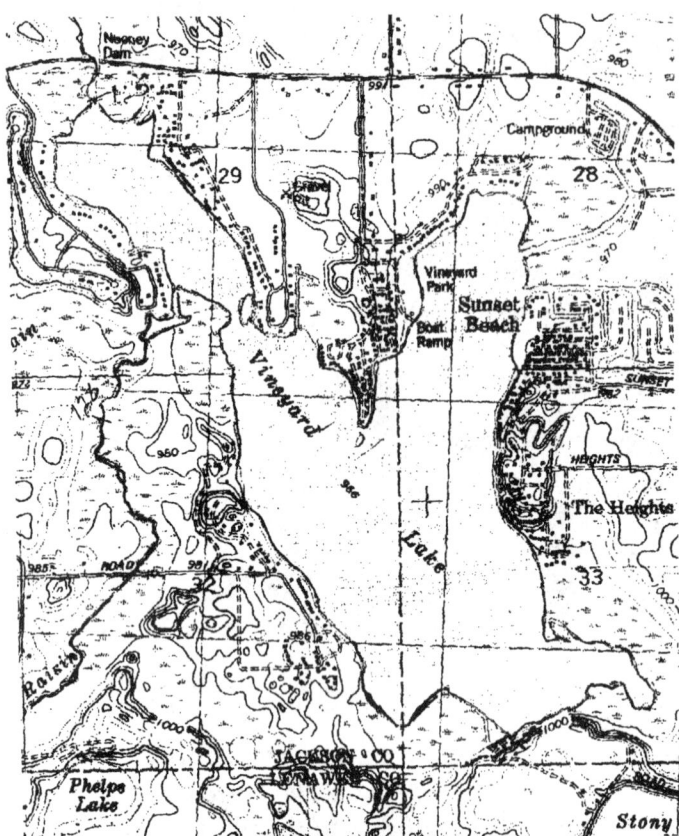

A 1980 survey map showing the cottage settlements around Vineyard Lake and Nooney Dam (upper left).

125.6-125 River enters Vineyard Lake about three-quarters of the way up the northeast shore. A number of subdivision plats including **The Heights** and **Sunset Beach** are located on the east shore. The elevation of the 505-acre Vineyard Lake is 966 feet.

124.8 Dam. The stream exits Vineyard Lake at its most northwesterly point near **Oakwood Beach**. Nooney Dam shows on some maps, but there is no discernible spillway at most water levels. It has been more recently described as the Vineyard Lake Level Control Structure, a one foot high dam designed to monitor the lake level.

124.9 Bridge. M-124 (Wampler Lake Road) crosses river east west.

124.15-123.4 Brooklyn Pond. A 16 acre pond is located behind the main business street of Brooklyn.

125.8 Plum Brook Drain enters the river from the west.

(Below) Boating on the Brooklyn Mill Pond about 1912.

Brooklyn to Manchester

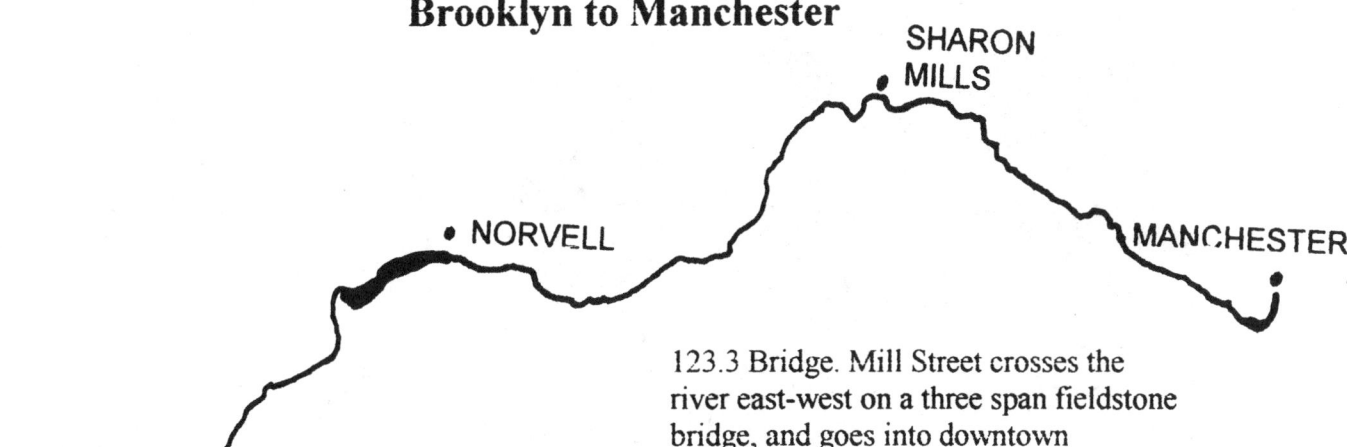

123.8 -123.1 **Brooklyn** The settlement which would become Brooklyn began in 1832 with the arrival of Calvin H. Swaine, a Baptist minister from New York state. The following year he built a sawmill and on July 28, 1834, became the first postmaster for **Swainesville.** Other settlers and investors included Chauncey Hawley, Lewis Cass and Israel Love. By ballot the name was changed to Brooklyn, after Brooklyn, New York, on October 25, 1836. It was incorporated as a village in 1879. The population was 1,176 in 2000 with a one square mile area.

123.4 Dam. A footbridge crosses the spillway at the Brooklyn dam which is 22 feet high. The large brick factory building at the site, was constructed in 1939 as one of the Ford community industries where Ford vehicle horn buttons and starter switches were manufactured 1945 to 1954, changing to plastic lamp lenses and armrests, 1954 to 1967. The plant, now closed, was owned and operated until 1989 by Industrial Automotive Products, a subsidiary of Jackson Gear.

123.3 Bridge. Mill Street crosses the river east-west on a three span fieldstone bridge, and goes into downtown Brooklyn.

122.95 Goose Creek enters from the west.

122.3 A small stream enters from the west

The Brooklyn dam and old Ford factory.

120.9 Bridge. Wolf Lake Road crosses the river northeast to southwest on a bridge of crumbling cement and steel.

120.2 Enter Norvell Township, Jackson County

119.6-120 A wide spot in the river, sometimes considered the upper end of Norvell Lake. It is where the water from Stony Lake, southwest of the community of Napoleon, enters the river.

119.4 Bridge. Austin Road crosses the short channel between the main section of Norvell Lake and a smaller, upper lake, in a northwest-southeast direction.

119.4 -118.2 Norvell Lake is 156 acres in size with the Village of Norvell on the northeast corner.

118.2 Dam. Elevation at the Norvell Lake spillway is 938 feet. The dam is 13 feet in height and the river is much smaller below the dam.

(Above) The Mill Street bridge in Brooklyn.

118.3 - 117.9 Norvell The first settler in Norvell was William Hunt who arrived in 1831. Harvey Austin was the first postmaster when the post office opened

The old mill mechanism can be seen below the dam at Norvell.

March 17, 1838. The settlement was named for John Norvell, the first U. S. senator for the State of Michigan. In 1878 it became a station on the Lake Shore & Michigan Southern Railroad.

118.1 Bridge. Mill Road crosses the spillway north-south. Beneath the bridge is the rusted mechanism and base of the old mill. Across the road a cobblestone monument carries a cornerstone with the year 1901.

117.6 A drain from a swampy area in the Sharonville State Wildlife Management Area enters the river from the north, having already picked up the outlet from Swezzey (variously spelled Sweezy or, on old maps Sweeney) Lake.

115.4 Bridge. Pierce Road crosses the river north-south in a woodsy area on a cement bridge built in 2001 by Jackson County.

114.9 Enter Manchester Township, Washtenaw County. The river at this point crosses only the extreme northwestern corner of Manchester Township.

114.6 The Norvell-Manchester Drain enters from the south.

114.25 Enter Sharon Township, Washtenaw County.

113.6 Sharon Valley Road crosses the river east west.

112.6 – 111.5 The 13-acre Sharon Mills reservoir has a elevation of 909 feet.

(Below) The restored Sharon Mills building with the later split fieldstone addition on the back. Explanatory panels are to the left of the main building..

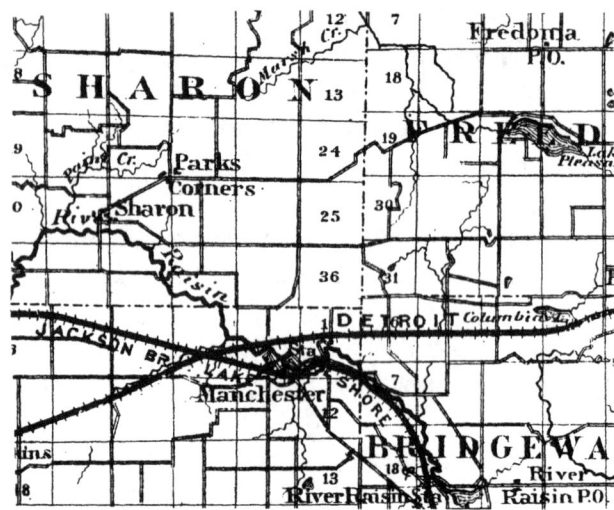

Sharon, with Parks Corners to the northeast, in 1873.

111.5 Sharon Hollow or Sharonville
There were a number of post offices at various times in Sharon Township. A post office which had operated since February of 1832 as **Richfield**, with Joseph O. Gilbert as the postmaster, changed its name to **Sharon** in January of 1836, and continued operation until July 15, 1855. The **Sharon Plain** post office opened June 24, 1867, with John Feather as postmaster, but operated only until September 18 of the same year. On December 14, 1891, the **Sharonville** post office was opened with Couch C. Dorr as the first postmaster and continued in operation until September 15, 1899. All of the post offices were named after Sharon Township which had been named for Sharon, Connecticut, when the township was organized in 1834. The hamlet of Sharonville is placed on modern maps where the east-west roads of Pleasant Lake and Bethel Church meet the Sharon Hollow Road, north of the River Raisin dam. It was the site of a Ford community industry 1939 to 1947 utilizing the old Sharon mill building. The plant produced cigar lighters, electrical switches and generator ammeters which measured the electricity in the battery. The old installation complete with landscaping has been restored by the Washtenaw County Parks and Recreation Commission. The grounds, with interpretive panels are open dawn to dusk, Memorial Day to Thanksgiving. In the summer there are also additional programs and tours.

111.5 Dam. Elevation of spillway is 911 feet.

111.5 Bridge. Sharon Hollow Road crosses the river north-south above the dam.

110 Bridge. Sharon Valley Road crosses east-west.

108.9 Enter Manchester Township, Washtenaw County

Manchester to Tecumseh

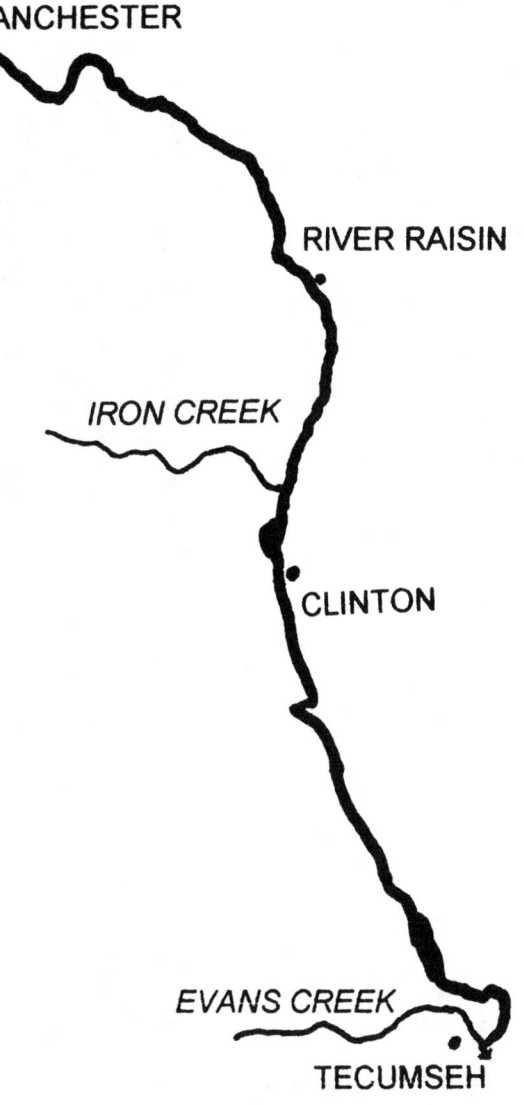

107.5-105.9 Manchester In 1833 John Gilbert received a grant of 400 acres and had it surveyed, but did not immediately settle on it. Later that year James Harvey Fargo, and his uncle, Steven Fargo, acting as the Manchester Milling Company, operated a sawmill and a grist mill. A post office was opened May 8, 1834, with Harry H. Gilbert as the first postmaster. Manchester was named after Manchester Township, Ontario County, New York. It was incorporated as a village in 1867. The population was 2,160 in 2000 with a land area of 1.9 square miles.

107 Bridge. Main Street, called Austin Road in the township, until 1925 known as Exchange Place, crosses the river southwest to northeast in downtown Manchester. The present bridge was reconstructed and dedicated 1972.

107 Dam. There is an 18 foot high dam under the bridge which contains an approximately 12 acre pond.

106.9 Bridge. Duncan Street crosses the river southwest to northeast

106.6 Closed Bridge. The old Furnace Street bridge which crosses the river, southwest to northeast. has been discontinued. Access is blocked by a chain link fence. An 1872 birds-eye view shows a foundry on the east side of the river at this point and the Case & Davis distillery on the west.

106.5 - 105.9 Manchester pond, about 45 acres. Near the east end of the pond there is an embankment which once carried the New York Central Railroad tracks across the water.

105.9 Dam. This area of town was earlier known as **Soulesville,** named after James Soules who built a sawmill nearby. Ford Motor Company built a plant on the site of an old grist mill in 1941 to manufacture ammeters for instrument clusters in automobiles. It was part of its community industry program, operated by Ford until 1957.

The dam is located under the bridge which carries the main street of Manchester over the River Raisin. A bridge has been located at this site for many years. This one is a modern reconstruction built in 1972, with colorful flower boxes in the summer.

However, the facilities continued to be used for manufacturing until the 1990s, and are still standing. The elevation of the dam spillway is 817 feet.

105.9 Bridge. Austin Road crosses the river east-west.

105.3 Bridge. The river flows south under Austin Road.

104.92 Enter Bridgewater Township, Washtenaw County.

102.15 Only a few pieces of foundation remain of the Wallace Road bridge which crossed the river east-west.

101.3 The outlet from Podunk Lake enters the river from the northeast.

101.2 Bridge. Wilder Road crosses the river east-west. A half mile west is the community of **River Raisin** (on some maps called **Raisin Basin**). There was a post office at this settlement which opened May 7, 1864, with Solomon Brown as the first postmaster. The office operated until 1902. The 1906 survey map places the community of River Raisin on both sides of Wilder Road, and a dam on the river just north of the road which created a small oddly-shaped lake labeled Raisin Basin.

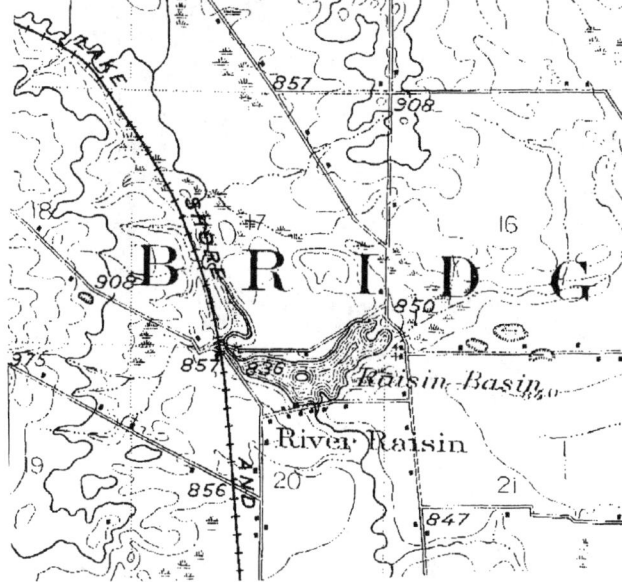

River Raisin showing a dam which forms a pond labeled Raisin Basin. From a 1906 survey map.

98.05 Bridge. Allen Road crosses east-west.

97.5 Iron Creek from Iron Mill Pond enters from the west.

97.4 – 96,9 Clinton Reservoir or Pond is about 118 acres in size. It is 812 feet in elevation.

96.9 Enter Clinton Township, Lenawee County

96.8 Atlas Mill Dam at Clinton, just south of the county line in the northwestern corner of Clinton, is about 13 feet in height. It is located at the western edge of the Water Wheel Community of homes and a favorite fishing spot. Near the road is the remnant of an old race which ran to the Clinton Woolen Mill, an industry which continued in the area until the 1950s and was known for its work supplying military uniforms to the U. S. government.

(Below) A 1907 view of the woolen mills at Clinton from the River Raisin near the U. S. 12 bridge.

(Above) Atlas dam in Clinton.

96.9 - 95 Clinton John Terrill visited the area seeking land in 1825, and returned in 1830 with Thaddeus Clark to settle. A post office opened October 8, 1831, with Horatio N. Baldwin as the first postmaster. The first census, in 1836, showed a population of 925. The town was named for DeWitt Clinton, who was instrumental in the building of the Erie Canal in New York state, making the westward trip easier and less expensive. Clinton was a station on the Lake Shore & Michigan Southern Railroad. It was incorporated as a village in 1838. In 2000 the population was 2,293 with an area of 1.5 square miles.

96.5 - 96. Floyd C. Tate Memorial Park is along the river south of U.S. 12. Facilities include restrooms, sports fields, playgrounds, and a wooded island in the river reached by footbridges from both banks

96.5 Bridge. U. S. 12 crosses the river east west through downtown Clinton.

93.8 Bridge. Staib Road crosses the river east-west. **Newburg** is just west of the river on the Newburg Highway. It was the site of a small rural post office which operated from April 29, 1891, when Helen L. McNeill was named the first postmaster, until 1909.

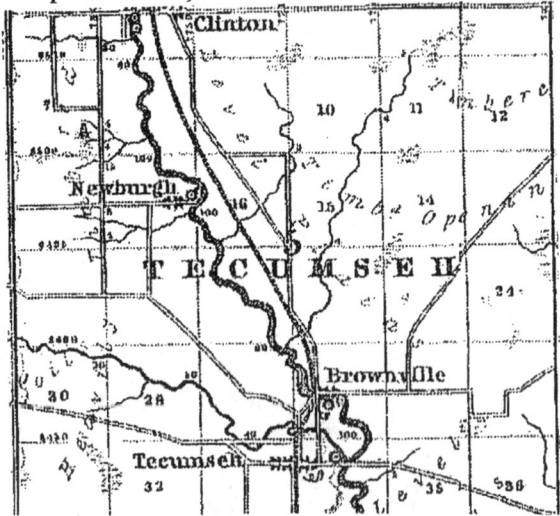

The village of Newburg from a map drawn about 1900. Note also that Tecumseh and Brownville are labeled as two separate communities.

Tecumseh to Blissfield

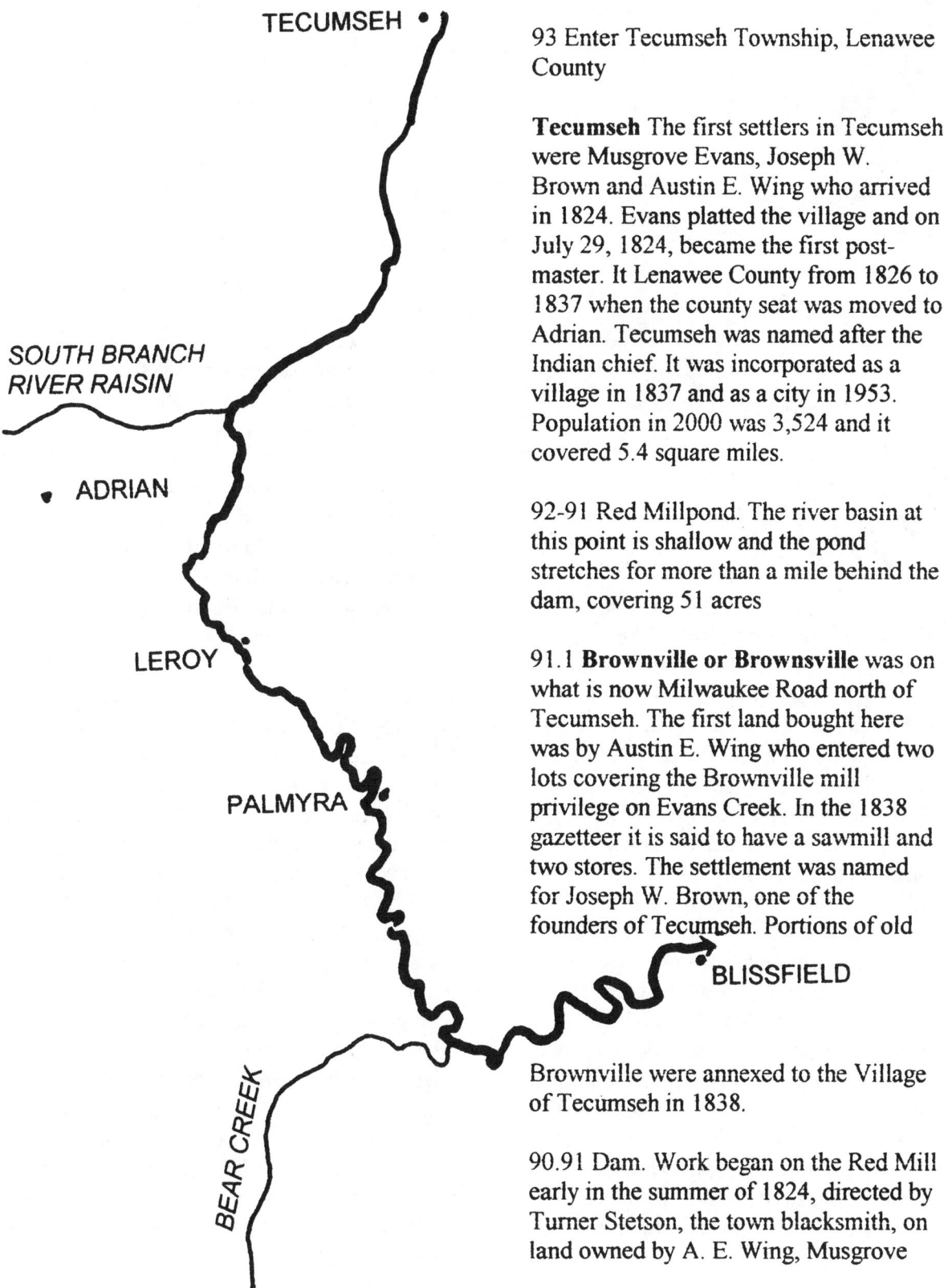

93 Enter Tecumseh Township, Lenawee County

Tecumseh The first settlers in Tecumseh were Musgrove Evans, Joseph W. Brown and Austin E. Wing who arrived in 1824. Evans platted the village and on July 29, 1824, became the first postmaster. It Lenawee County from 1826 to 1837 when the county seat was moved to Adrian. Tecumseh was named after the Indian chief. It was incorporated as a village in 1837 and as a city in 1953. Population in 2000 was 3,524 and it covered 5.4 square miles.

92-91 Red Millpond. The river basin at this point is shallow and the pond stretches for more than a mile behind the dam, covering 51 acres

91.1 **Brownville or Brownsville** was on what is now Milwaukee Road north of Tecumseh. The first land bought here was by Austin E. Wing who entered two lots covering the Brownville mill privilege on Evans Creek. In the 1838 gazetteer it is said to have a sawmill and two stores. The settlement was named for Joseph W. Brown, one of the founders of Tecumseh. Portions of old Brownville were annexed to the Village of Tecumseh in 1838.

90.91 Dam. Work began on the Red Mill early in the summer of 1824, directed by Turner Stetson, the town blacksmith, on land owned by A. E. Wing, Musgrove

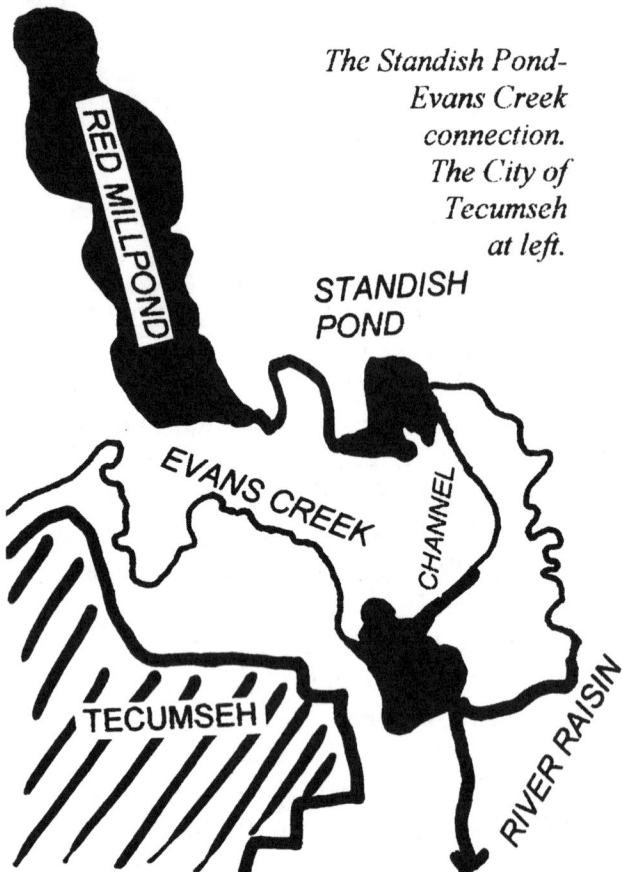

The Standish Pond-Evans Creek connection. The City of Tecumseh at left.

Evans and Joseph W. Brown. The first mill was located just north of the Brownsville bridge. The grist mill was built in 1826 on the south side of the river opposite the sawmill and used the same water power, the water reaching its wheel through a wooden flume. Millstones were procured locally, by splitting a granite boulder found northeast of the settlement. The boulder had been broken by the action of a forest fire and it was discovered that its interior texture was just right for grinding. The public gathered to cheer the first public grinding of wheat on the 4th of July, 1826. In 1902 the dam was acquired by George U. Smith and Louis Schneider who built a brick building at the end of the race on the north side of the bridge to feed water-driven turbines which would provide electricity for the Tecumseh area. The installation was sold to Consumers Power which continued the operation until 1950.

90.91 Bridge. Tecumseh Highway crosses the river north-south.

90.4 - 90.2 **Standish Pond**. In the late 1830s Stillman Blanchard, operating as the Globe Milling Company, bought all the land from Burt Street south to the La Plaisance Bay Road, 600 acres in all, encompassing the flood plains of the two streams. He built a flour mill on the Chicago Highway with a mill pond on Evans Creek. However, at that point the bed of the river is much lower than that of the creek so, in order to use all the water it was necessary to raise the river level. This was done by building a dam near Burt Street, forming what is known as Standish Pond, and digging a long ditch from it around the intervening hills to convey the high river water to the creek basin. Standish Pond has a 13.5 foot dam and covers 13 acres.

The sawmill part of the project was built partially to process lumber for the other construction. Its race was dug along the north shore of the river and directly through the circle and square of the ancient Indian Dancing Ground. By the time the new grist mill was ready to run in 1839, the panic of 1837 had doomed the project. It struggled until 1858 when it was sold to satisfy the mortgage. The purchaser was an experienced miller and with good management, a fine crop of wheat and the demand caused by the Civil War, the operation prospered. Globe Milling Company flour was distributed worldwide, even to India in tin containers. Later the Hayden Mill was constructed on the south side of the pond, using a race which funneled water under the dam.

Two views of the Tecumseh dam below Red Mill pond taken about a hundred years apart. (Top) A horse and wagon cross the "new bridge" in 1909. (Below) Cars and flowers on the modern bridge photographed in 2008.

A waterwheel still turns on the side of the old Hayden Mill building at Tecumseh.

The 1898 mill building was restored by Ford as a community industry opening in 1935 to process soybeans for use in plastics. It was closed in 1948 and since then has been used for a number of community purposes. The front of the structure displays a working waterwheel.

89.6 Dam. Evans Creek enters the river from the northwest. It is named for Musgrove Evans, one of the founders of Tecumseh. At this point the waters behind the dam are those of Evans Creek, supplemented by the River Raisin flow through Standish Pond. The Evans Creek spillway level is 760 feet, with a 22.3 foot dam.

89.5 Bridge. Chicago Boulevard crosses the river east-west. **Indian Crossing**, a Tecumseh City Park, is at the intersection.

88.1 Enter Raisin Township, Lenawee County

88.1 Bridge. Russell Road crosses the river east-west on a bridge first constructed in 1978.

87.5 A bridge which formerly carried Mill Highway to meet Comfort Road across the river is no longer in operation.

83.2 Bridge. Sutton Road crosses east-west on a bridge constructed in 1960.

82.55 Bridge. Raisin Center Highway crosses north-south. The small community of Raisin Center is about a mile south, near the old railroad trackbed on Chase Road.

Raisin Center was settled in 1831 and a Quaker meeting house erected in 1834. A post office was opened June 9, 1868 with Stephen Galloway as the first postmaster. When the Lake Shore & Michigan Southern Railroad came through in 1878, it established a station called **Chase's.** The post office closed in 1902. A prominent feature of the community today is the old Raisin Center Friends Cemetery.

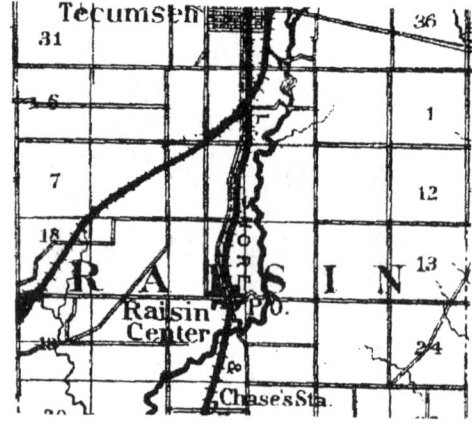

Raisin Center and nearby Chase's Station, on an 1872 map.

82.5 Railroad Bridge. An old Penn Central bridge crosses north-south

(Above) The railroad bridge at Leroy reflected in a quiet river.

80.8 Bridge. Wilmoth Road crosses the river north-south.

78.7 South Branch of Raisin River enters the river about a two and a half miles northeast of the City of Adrian. The South Branch rises near Clayton in Hudson Township Lenawee County and flows east and south, picking up Harrison Drain, Hazen Creek, and Stony Creek, near the settlement of Sand Creek in Madison Township, before turning northeast in the City of Adrian, which it bisects. North of Adrian the South Branch is joined by Beaver Creek and Harkness Drain before entering the main river north of Laberdee Road.

Adrian (on south branch of the River Raisin) in Adrian Township, Lenawee County. was founded by Addison Comstock and his father, Darius, who went in 1825 to Detroit, then Tecumseh and asked Musgrove Evans and Joseph Brown where might be a good place to settle. They recommended looking south and west of Tecumseh. Darius bought 640 acres in **"Pleasant Valley"** (a little east of M-52 and Valley Road).

Le Roy on a map about 1844. Just south of the settlement the Erie and Kalamazoo Railroad goes by on the way to Adrian.

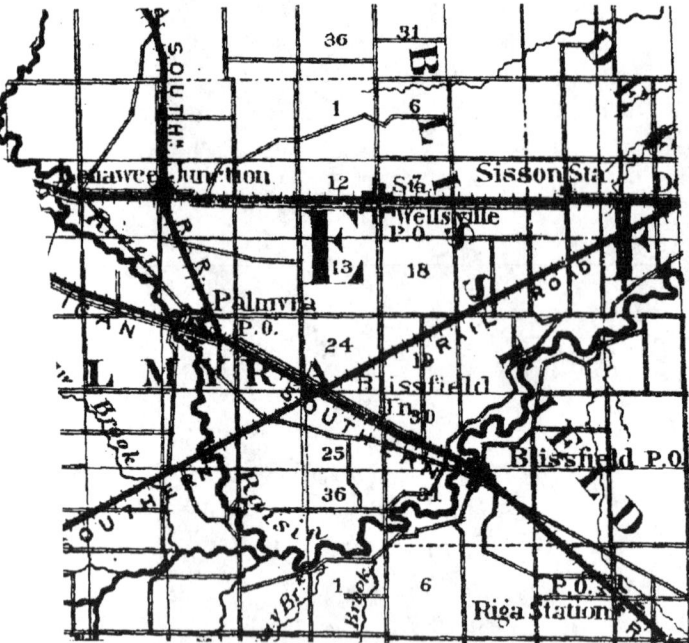

This 1873 map shows Lenawee Junction north of Palmyra, and Blissfield Junction northwest of the Village of Blissfield.

Addison found his land near a spring on the east side of the south branch of the River Raisin (today just east of the Maumee Street bridge). In 1827 they returned and built a sawmill just north of the spring. In 1829 Addison Comstock and Isaac Deane built a grist mill downstream from the sawmill. Island Park, in the River Raisin south branch, began in 1934 and is reached by a little footbridge. In 1836 the Erie and Kalamazoo Railroad ran the first train in the Northwest Territory from Toledo to Adrian. It was first powered by horses, changed every four miles, but a few months later it was converted to steam. The population of Adrian in 2000 was 21,574 with an area of 7.3 square miles.

78.2 Laberdee Road crosses on a 1958 Lenawee County-built bridge.

78. Large Island left by old ox-bow.

76.8 Enter Palmyra Township, Lenawee County.

76.3 Bridge. Academy Road crosses the river east-west. There is an old gaging station nearby.

73.6 Railroad bridge. Penn Central crosses east-west.

Le Roy or Leroy On an 1844 map of the area there is a small settlement called Le Roy near the railroad bridge. The 1838 gazetteer notes that Leroy has "a store, and sawmill, and a flouring mill erecting. It is passed by the State road from Toledo to Adrian." From this point a ridge goes off to the northeast. According to an 1844 map "This ridge is from 10 to 20 feet high, the former boundary of the lake shore, composed of sand and gravel."

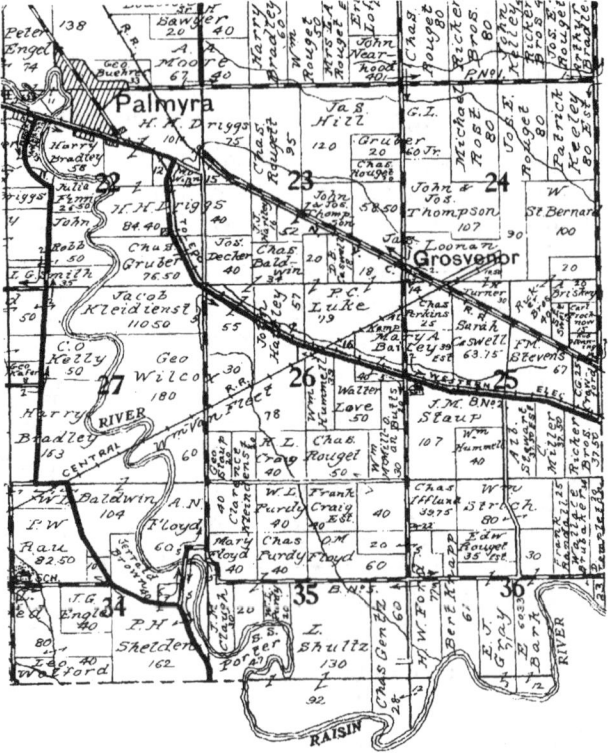

The boundary between Palmyra and Ogden townships follows the River Raisin near the southeast corner.

73.5 Bridge. Deerfield Road crosses east-west and enters Adrian on the west. A mile and a half east on the Deerfield Road is the small settlement of **Lenawee Junction,** where two railroad tracks cross. The tracks still form a junction at this point, but the switch is automated and only a few residences remain nearby to represent the old community.

69-68.7 **Palmyra** The settlement was founded in 1827 by Timothy B. Goff, who named it after his hometown in New York. The first post office opened March 27, 1833, with Alexander R. Tiffany as the first postmaster. The settlement was a station on the Lake Shore & Michigan Southern Railroad.

68.7 Bridge. U. S. 223 crosses the river southeast to northwest.

65.3 Railroad bridge. Railroad crosses river and goes into **Grosvenor** on the east.

64.2 Bridge. Crockett Road crosses the river north south. Elevation at the bridge is 696 feet.

62.1 From this point to the east township line the river forms the boundary between Palmyra Township on the north bank and Ogden Township on the south bank.

61.6 Black Creek enters from the southwest having already picked up Bear Creek, Hahn Drain, Walker Brook, and Gleason Brook. On the earliest French maps the river which entered Lake Erie near Frenchtown was called *Riviere aux Ours* or Bear River. Most of the old maps also show a stream which rises in the south, arches north and then curves slightly south again before it enters Lake Erie. This is the configuration which would occur if Bear Creek, which joins Black Creek just before its junction with the Raisin, was considered the main river's primary source.

60.4 Bay Drain enters from the south

58.6 Enter Blissfield Township, Lenawee County. At this point the township boundary leaves the river and drops four-tenths of a mile south to the surveyor's line.

58.4 Clemente Drain enters from the south.

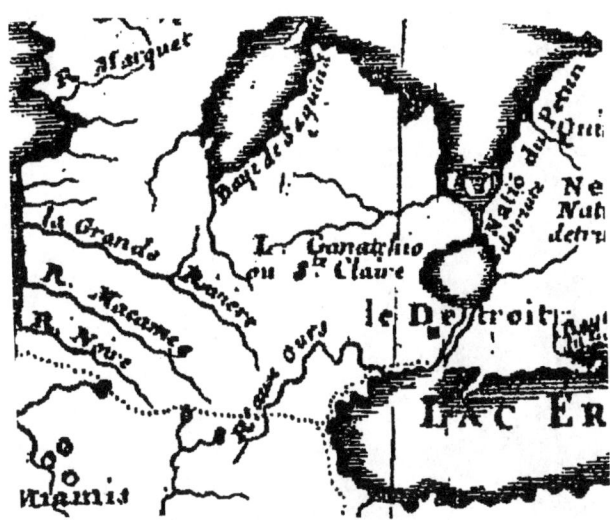

On this 1703 French map the river which exits into Lake Erie is called the "R. aux Ours" or Bear River and seems to indicate that the mapmaker saw Bear Creek as the main stream of the River Raisin.

13792E6 The Old Mill Dam River Raisin, Blissfield, Mich. Lenardson Bros. & Co., Publishers.

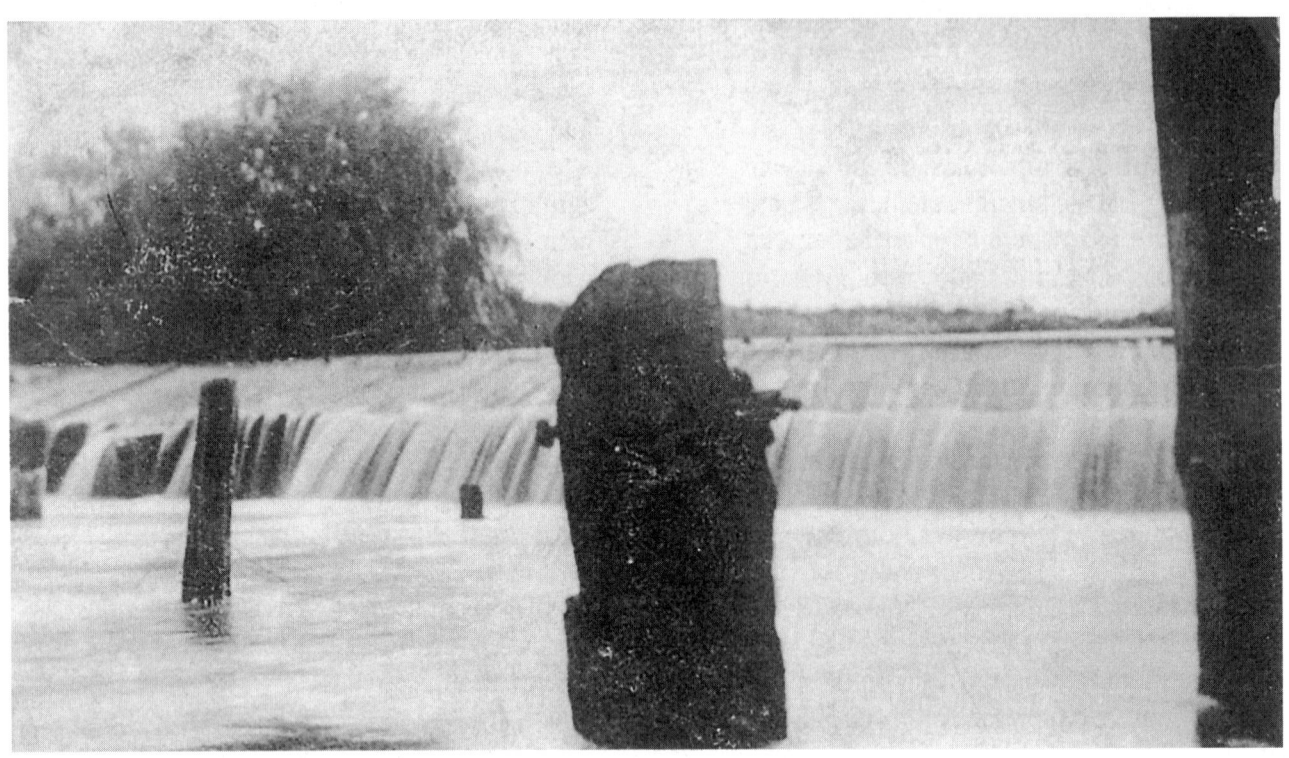

Blissfield a century ago. (Above) The old mill dam on a 1908 postcard. (Below) A view of the River Raisin at Blissfield, looking north.

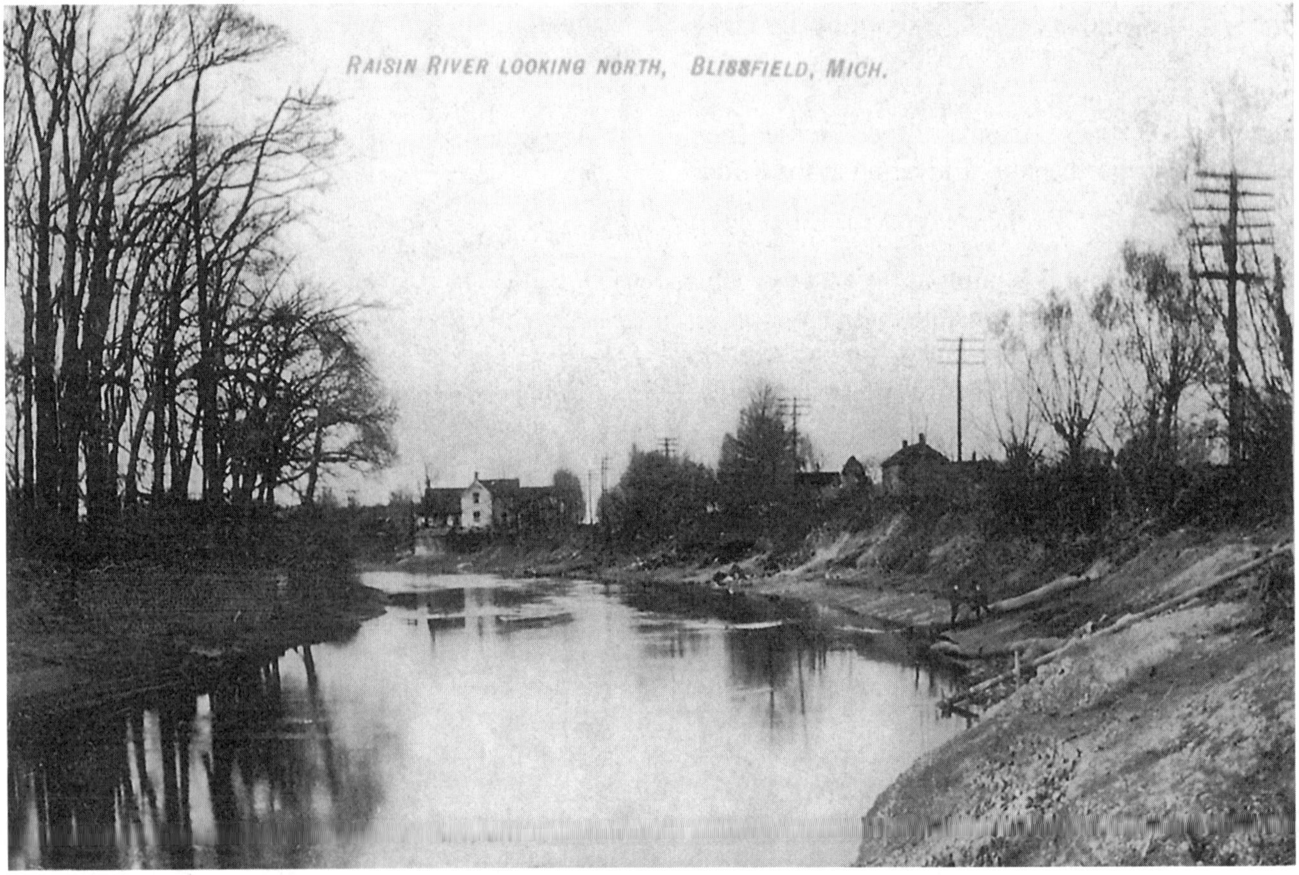

Blissfield to Dundee

56.3 Little evidence remains of a dam some old maps show on Pearl Street.

57.5- 54.85- **Blissfield** William Kedzie, of Delhi, New York, made the first government purchase of land here where a ford made the River Raisin easy to cross, but did not settle until the fall of 1861. Hervey Bliss, from Monroe County, bought land in June of 1824 and arrived to stay in December. George Giles began about 1826 to tame the swamps of the area. The Great Black Swamp near Toledo extended west to Blissfield. As part of that effort Giles cut a road 13 miles along the River Raisin from Petersburg to Blissfield. By 1834 he had a three story inn in Blissfield for pioneers passing through, and a canoe which could transport the pioneers and their belongings across the river. To increase the flow of pioneers through Blissfield, he also cut a six mile road through the swamps southeast, and got the state to build a log causeway through the swamps. This led to the establishment of the first drainage district in Michigan. Blissfield Township was organized in 1827. A post office called Blissfield opened on March 28, 1838, with Hervey Bliss as postmaster. Blissfield was incorporated as a village in 1875. In 2000 the population was 3,223 with an area of 2.1 square miles. The annual Blissfield River Raisin Festival celebrated its 25th anniversary in 2008.

56.4 – 55.6 On the east side of the bridge is the 17-acre **Ellis Park**, named for A. D. Ellis proprietor of a dry goods store, and once president of the village council. He gave land to the village in 1919 for use as a park with the provision that there be "No Sunday base ball, no liquor, no questionable amusements (like circuses) on the grounds." Facilities include a canoe launch, shuffleboard, volleyball courts, a swimming pool,

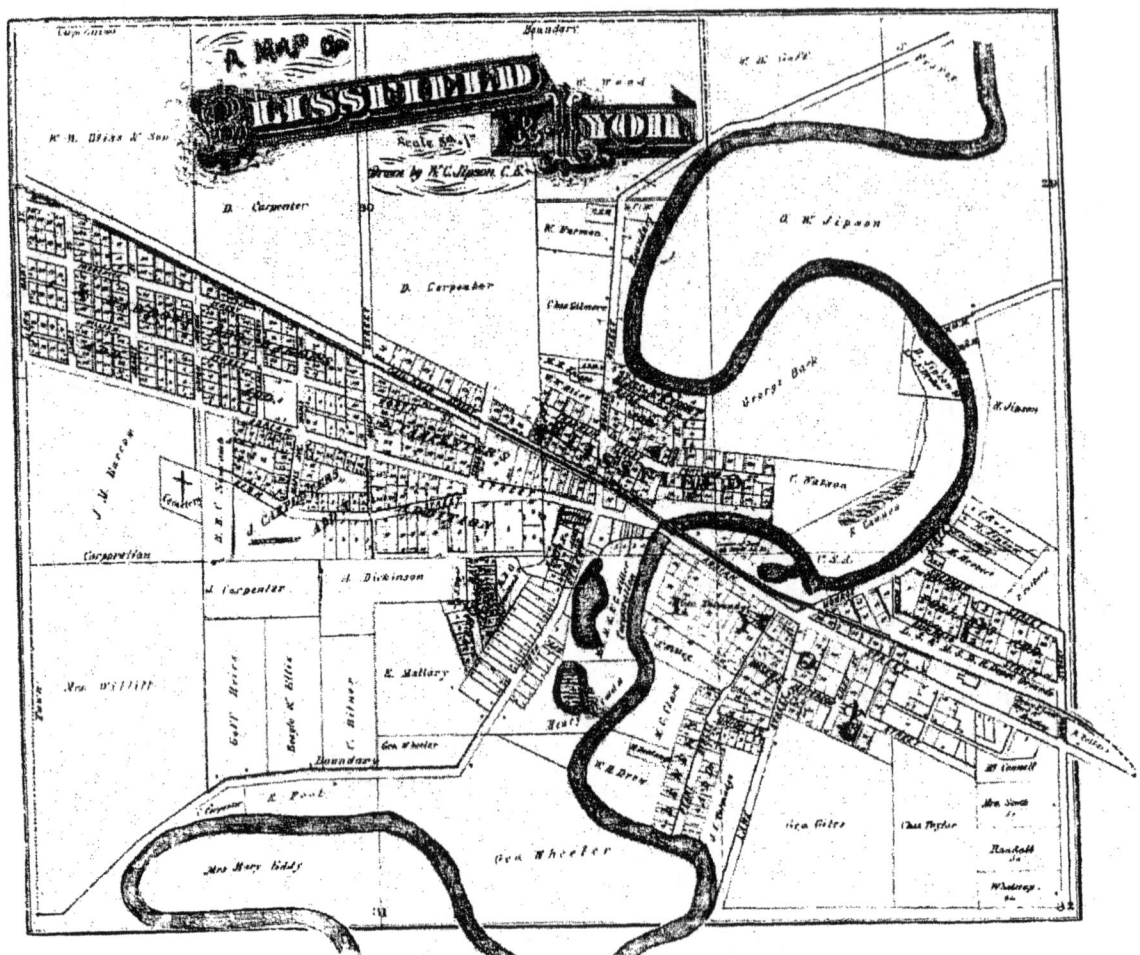

picnic tables and shelters and athletic fields.

55.9 - 55.2 Lyons or Lyons Before the river was actually bridged at this point, the two communities across from each other at the ford developed separately. The first settler on the east side of the bridge was George Giles who came in 1826 and built the first hotel. By 1874 there was a water-powered flour mill on the east side.

56 – 55.6 On the west side of the river is seven-acre **Clara Bachmayer Park**, on land donated by her widower, Joseph Bachmayer. Facilities include playgrounds and picnic tables and a shelter. Two picturesque pedestrian bridges link Bachmayer Park with Ellis Park across the river.

(Above) Blissfield, on the west side of the River Raisin and Lyon on the east side, from the 1874 Lenawee County atlas. Today the major part of the business section is west of the river.

55.6 Bridge U.S. 223, Adrian Street, crosses the river southeast-northwest through downtown Blissfield. This is the site of the famous triple bridges. Originally the Lake Shore Railroad tracks ran on the northern bridge, the wagon and pedestrian bridge was to the south, and in 1901 the Toledo and Western Railroad built a crossing in the middle. Today three bridges still stand but the modern railroad runs on the northernmost one, the highway bridge is in the middle, and the bridge on the south is for pedestrian traffic.

(Above) A modern rendition of Blissfield's famous triple bridge crossing. The bridges today are: from the top, a modern railroad bridge, for cars and other motor vehicles, and, the newest of the three, at right, for pedestrians.

54.9 Dam. An old dam built before 1900 for a sugar beet processing plant was also used for electric power. In 1912 the sugar beet company and village council decided to erect a more substantial steel and concrete dam about 10 feet in height. The electric power plant was sold to Consumers Power in 1950. The water crossing the dam today rolls over slanted concrete, usually not deep enough to float even a small boat, and drops to scattered rocks at its base. It is a hazard for boaters and a sign, designed to hang over the river at the old dam, reads:

**Do not cross dam
3 have died
Portage Around**

50.3 Wiley Drain enters from the northwest.

50.25 Camp Drain enters from the north having already merged with Brenott Drain

49.8 Several large islands are in the river just below Slager Road, the result of an old ox-bow.

There is a space of more than 15 miles, 55.6 to 40.4, Blissfield to Deerfield, where there are no bridges over the river.

49.3 Floodwood Creek enters from the south having already picked up Riga Drain.

48.6 Enter Deerfield Township, Lenawee County

44.8 Kellar Drain enters from the south.

40.5 - 40.3 **Deerfield** William Kedzie, the earliest land purchaser in Blissfield, also bought land in the Deerfield area in 1824. He came to settle in 1826 and was named the first postmaster when a post office called **Kedzie's Grove** opened on March 20, 1828. The name of the post office and settlement was changed to Deerfield in 1837, noting the large number of deer in the area. Deerfield was incorporated as a village in 1873. The population in 2000 was 1,005 with an area of .9 square miles.

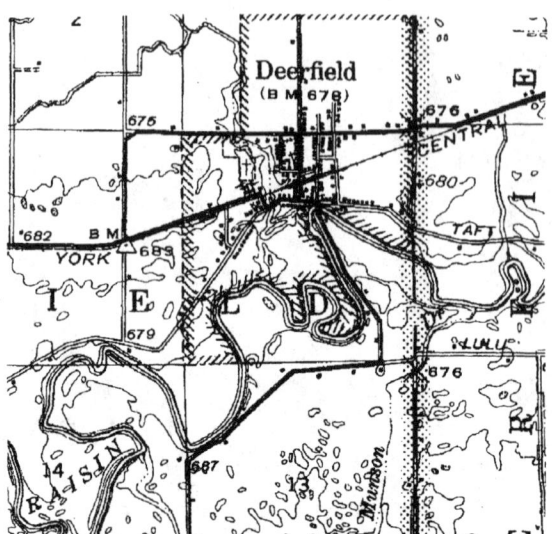

40.45 Island in river

Deerfield from an old survey map.

40.4 Bridge. Road crosses the river north-south on a cement and steel bridge and enters Deerfield connecting with Bucholtz Road in the township. The earliest bridge at this site was built in 1834. It was replaced by a covered bridge in 1864, an iron structure in 1903 and the present concrete bridge in 1953. A grist mill was built near this site as early as 1830, and later an electric power plant. Wooden dams did not hold well, and a steel dam was built but proved unprofitable due to low water levels. Water forced its way around the steel structure, but it was later salvaged.

39.8 Enter Summerfield Township, Monroe County

(Below) The Blissfield dam in 2008.

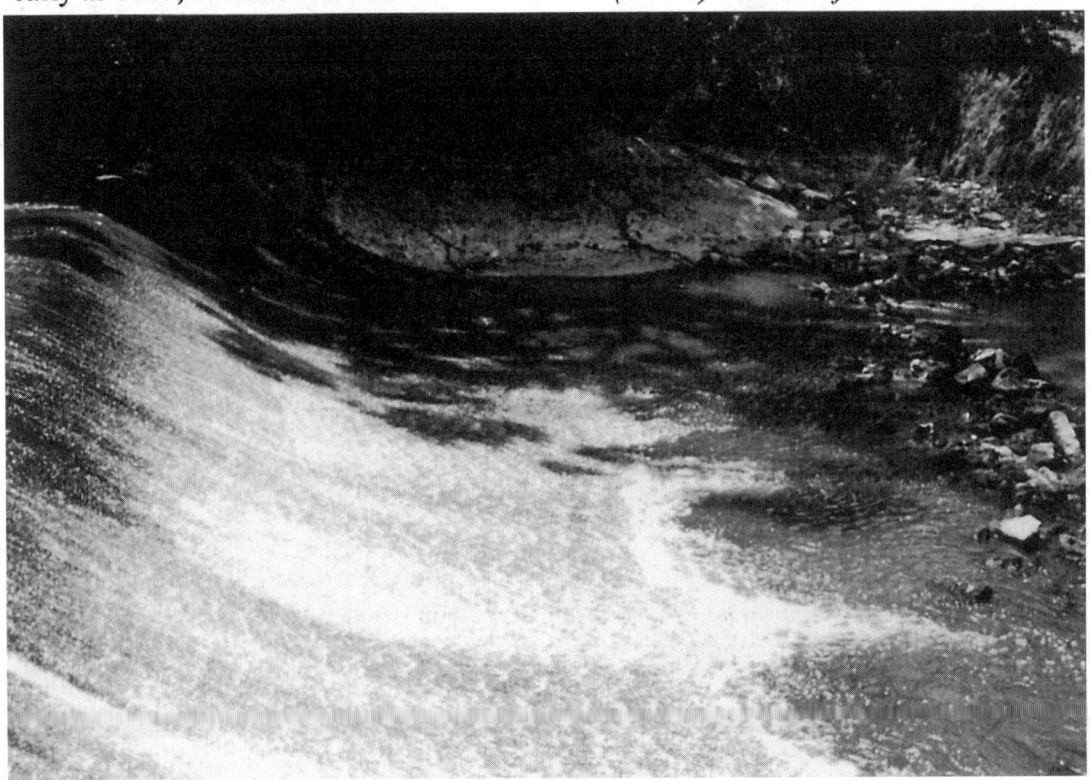

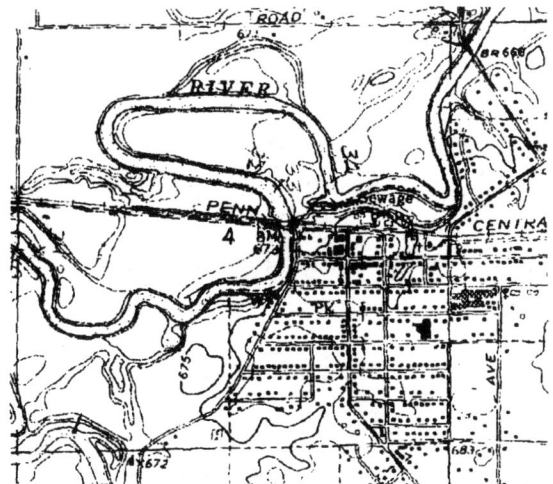

Petersburg took advantage of a natural curve in the river to build a mill race. This bend begins at the upper left of the village map below.

37 Burton and White Drain enters from the south.

35.8 Russel Drain enters from the South.

32.7 Miller Drain enters from the west.

33.4- 31.5 Petersburg Richard Peters started a farm near this place in 1824 and became its first postmaster when a post office called **Summerfield** opened in April of 1831. The name was changed to Petersburgh in 1863, and to Petersburg in 1893. Peters sold a portion of his land

(Below) A plat of Petersburgh from an 1870s atlas.

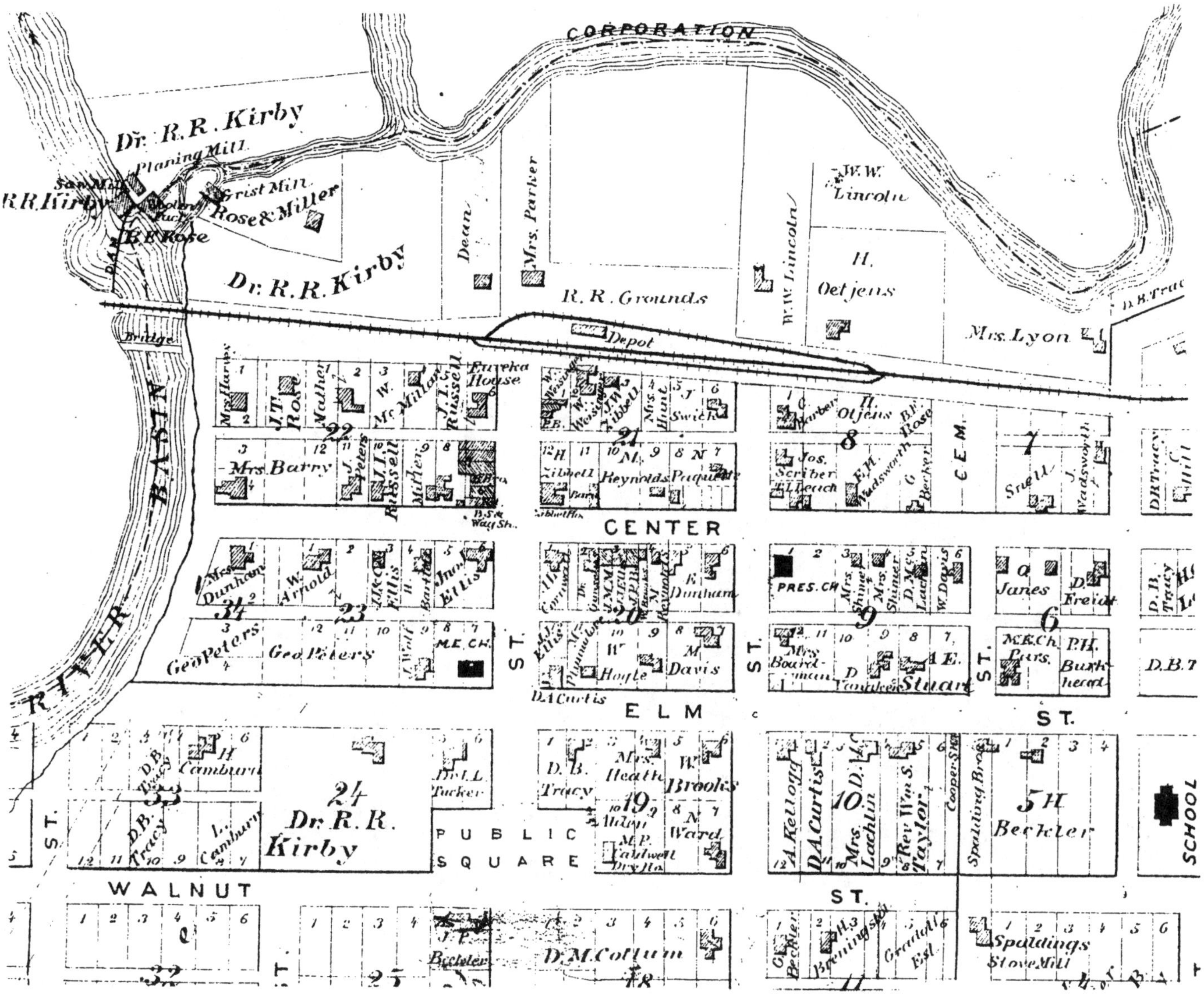

to Thomas G. Cole and Austin E. Wing of Monroe, who established a settlement. Petersburg was incorporated as a village in 1869 and as a city in 1967. In 2000 it had a population of 1,167 and was .5 square miles in area.

By the time the river reached Petersburg it could be a real obstacle. William Kedzie later said that when he first came to Deerfield in 1827 there was no bridge at Petersburg. The gristmill, sawmill, blacksmith, store and doctor were all at Monroe, 25 miles away. To cross the river at Petersburg he had to ferry the grist across the river in a large canoe, take his wagon apart and use the canoe to get it over the river, and make the horses swim across the water. After he had reassembled his wagon and hitched up the team he was ready to proceed. The same operation was necessary on the return trip.

33.13 Bridge. Deerfield Road crosses the river east-west.

33.14 Railroad bridge. Penn Central tracks cross east-west.

31.4 Petersburg Road crosses the river southeast to northwest.

31.35 Enter Dundee Township, Monroe County.

31.3 Roe Drain enters from the northwest.

28.5 Stacy Drain enters from the south.

24.8 Dunlap Drain enters from the southwest.

24.5 Little Raisin Creek enters the river from the northwest, just below the Maple Grove Cemetery.

23.7 Bridge. U. S. 23, crosses north-south

(Below) "Boating on the Raisin," a postcard from about 1910.

Dundee to Lake Erie

22.65 Dundee dam. The first dam, a simple brush structure, may have been built at this point as early as 1827, it was later improved with large timbers. In 1909 in an effort to supply not only the grist mill, but an electric power plant, a

23.3 – 22 **Dundee**. William Remington made the first land entry and Riley Ingersoll arrived from New York State to be the first settler in 1824. About 1830 S. Van Ness platted a village he called **Van Ness's Mills**. In 1836 the **Winfield** post office was moved to the village and the name of both post office and village became Dundee, named after the township which had been named for Dundee, Scotland. Dundee was incorporated as a village in 1855. Population in 2000 was 3,522, with a land area of 3.2 square miles.

(Below) Dundee mill and the timber dam from a 1906 postcard. Three years later, in 1909 a new concrete dam was erected at this point.

OLD MILL, DUNDEE, MICH.

new concrete dam was constructed at this point. This was the structure that Henry Ford bought in 1934 and improved to furnish power to a village industries factory which supplied Ford Motor Company with copper tips for welding machines. A stone addition to the building was made from stone blasted from the river bed near the base of the dam. The small factory was taken out of production in 1954 and sold to Wolverine Manufacturing and Fabricating Company, which continued work in the refurbished mill building until 1970, when the building and 13.8 acres were donated to the Village of Dundee. Today there is a museum of the area in the mill building, where Henry Ford's old turbine is still on display. A small park occupies the mill grounds upstream from the dam.

22.6 Bridge. M-50, called Tecumseh Street in town, and Custer Drive in the township, crosses the river northwest-southeast and enters Dundee. By 1833 seven major Michigan roads converged

(Below) A map of Dundee before 1900 with a cheese factory near the mill.

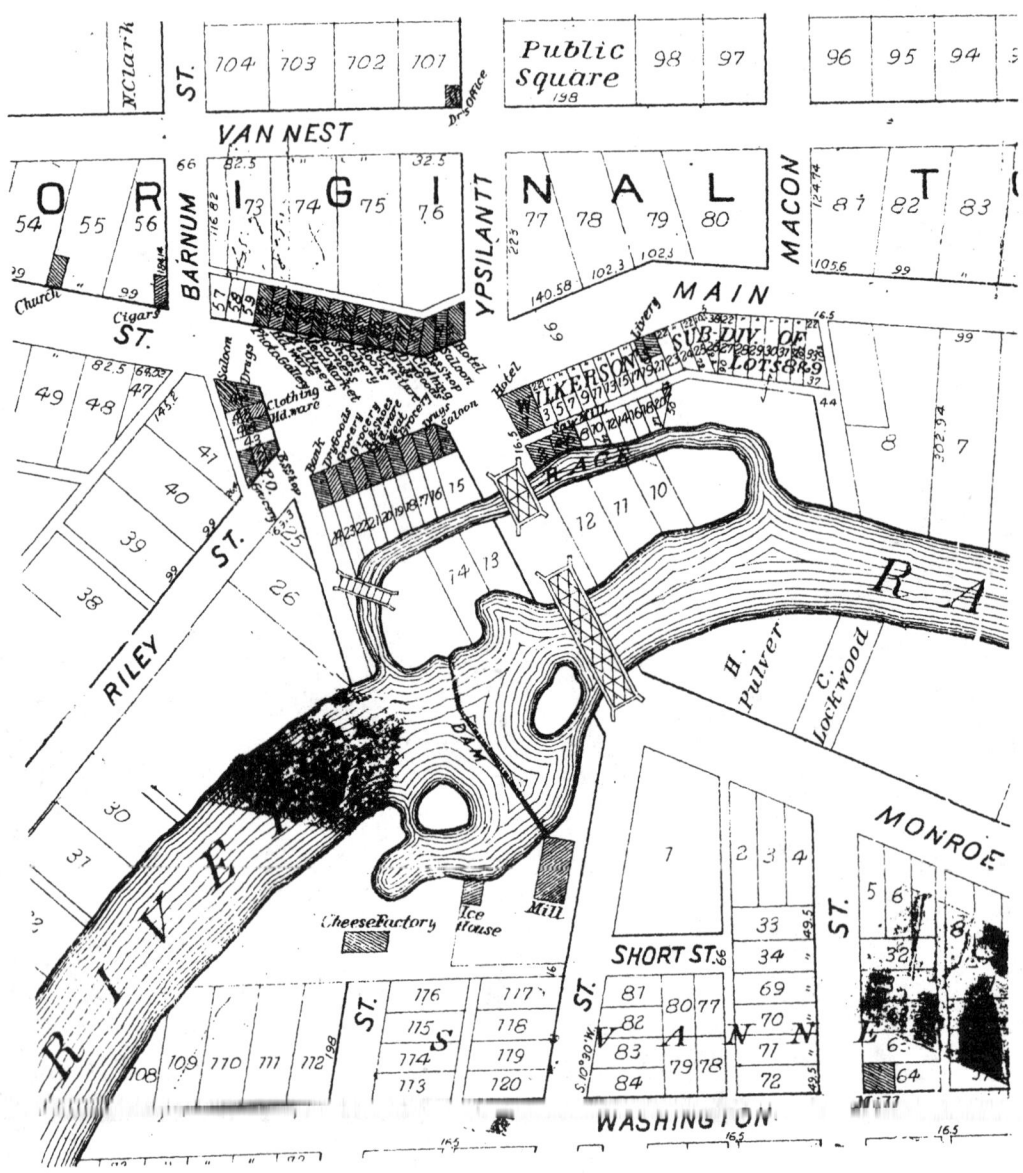

at the Dundee crossing of the River Raisin and there was a toll bridge erected at that point. There are lookouts, gardens and other park facilities at all four corners of the present bridge.

22.17 Railroad bridge. An old Ann Arbor Railroad track crosses the river north-south near the southern boundary of Dundee.

21.3 **Winfield**. According to old histories "about two miles east of Dundee" a post office was opened in the home of the first postmaster John H. Montgomery on May 2, 1834, and called Winfield. On January 11, 1836, Alonzo Curtis was named postmaster and the post office moved to Dundee, the name being changed to Dundee.

18.3 Macon Creek enters the river from the northwest. It flows from the west with its three distinct branches uniting northwest of Dundee. A short distance up this creek the Dundee Cement Company plant was built in 1957, a major employer in southeastern Michigan. This is the area of an old Indian reservation, and the river was named for an old chief who once lived on its banks.

17.4 Saline River enters from the north. The river rises in Washtenaw County and passes through the cities of Saline and Milan. It was named for the salt springs just upstream from its junction with the River Raisin.

15.8 Enter Raisinville Township, Monroe County.

15.65 Railroad bridge. Detroit, Toledo and Ironton Railroad crosses southwest-northeast.

Hamlin Post Office and Raisinville Station from a plat map drawn about 1890.

14.7 **Hamlin**. Old maps show a settlement called Hamlin on the north bank of the river just south of the road. The settlement was named after Hannibal Hamlin, vice-president of the United States 1861-1865. A post office named Hamlin opened March 28, 1862, with Calvin Clark as first postmaster. The Chicago and Southern Canada Railway had a station just north of Hamlin. Some records indicate that the name of the post office was changed to Raisinville in 1876, however a map from about 1900 shows **Raisinville Station** and Hamlin P.O. at the same location.

14.5 French Claims. Here the plat maps of the area change from regularly laid out townships to diagonal lines marking narrow lots on either side of the river. Settlement inland to this point, largely by French settlers, preceded the surveying of the land. Using the French custom they laid out long "ribbon" farms, with a narrow riverfront and extending away from the river, sometimes over a mile, until a swamp or some other obstacle was reached. These

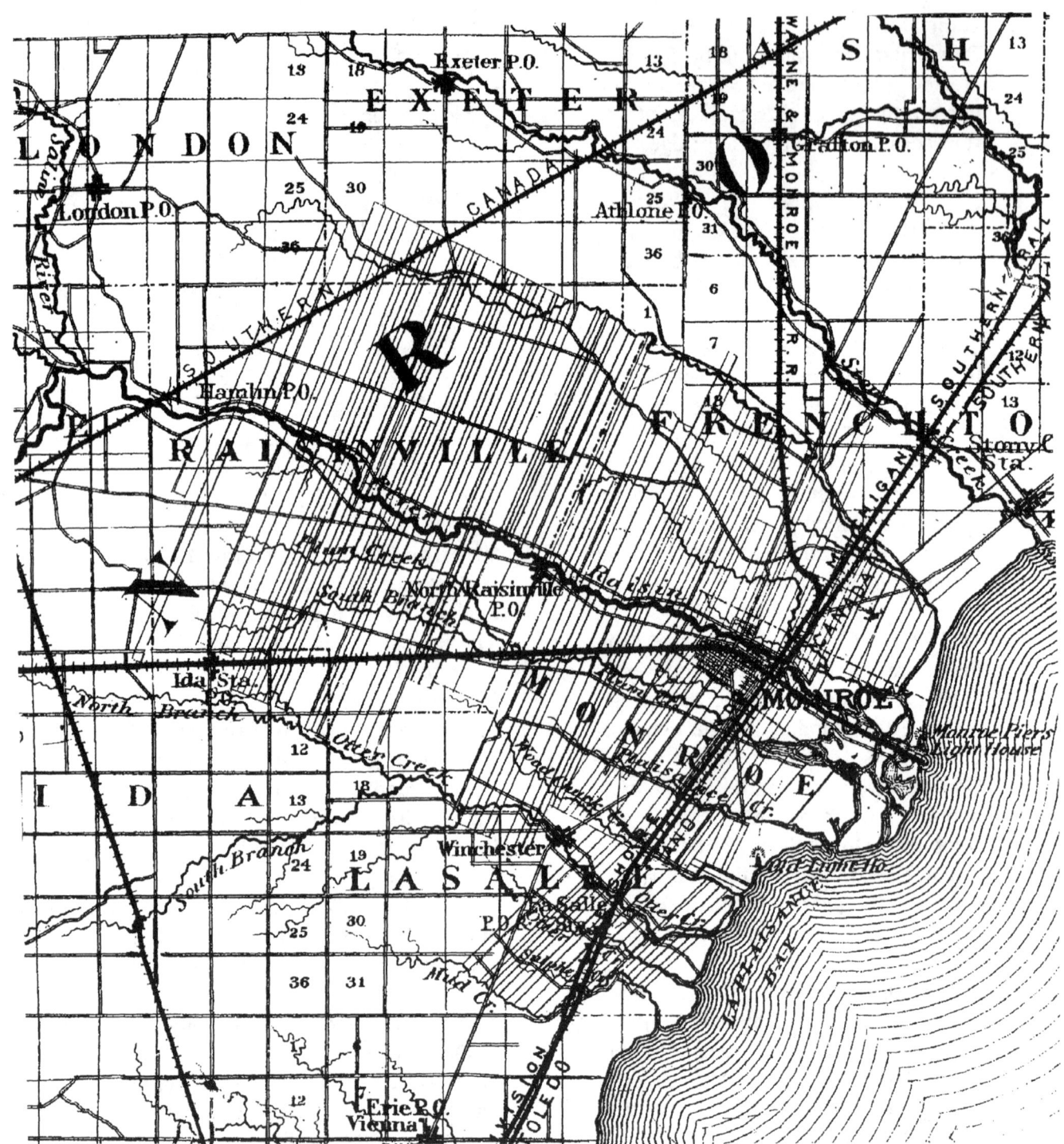

Right after the Dundee – Raisinville Township line the regular square lots and roads give way to diagonal "ribbon farms." These land boundaries, which exist even today, are the result of land purchases from the Indians, and those between the early French settlers being laid out before the regular townships were surveyed. Settlers built their houses on the river with the farm stretching out behind until it met a natural obstacle. It was told that the houses were close enough together that they could shout from one house to the next and form a sort of human telegraph relay.

claims, largely purchased (or in some instances they were gifts) from the Indians, or each other, were major headaches for the Surveyor General when the land office was officially set up in the 1820s and continue to cause trouble for modern day surveyors. Although, as Indian agent C. Jouett wrote Washington in 1803 "disputes have frequently arisen relative to their titles; and those disputes have always terminated by an adjudication in favor of the oldest Indian deed."

13.4 **Murciak Dam**. A dam six feet in height contains a one acre pond.

13.18 **Bruckner Bridge**. Ida Maybee Road (the road between Ida, to the south, and Maybee on the north) crosses the river southwest to northeast. About a half mile to the south is the **Bridge School**, the first public school in the State of Michigan. It was formed to "provide a building and financial support for basic education." The first building was constructed in 1828, the present brick building was erected in 1868. Now, many times enlarged, it serves as the Raisinville Township Hall.

The River Raisin is a sparkling stream in the woods just past Murciak Dam.

12.8 **Grape** Just east of the bridge the small residential settlement of Grape

(At right) The school in the center was the first "free" school in the state. To the right are the lime kilns and post office of Grape, although the community is not named on this map.

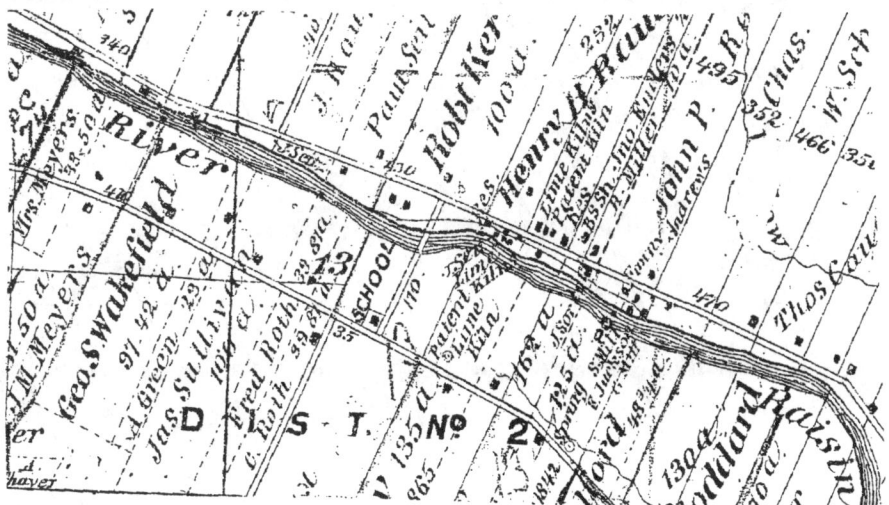

(named for the same grapevines that gave the river its French name) spreads along Custer Road north of the river. A post office named Grape opened here on June 1, 1887, with Hannah W. Atkinson as the first postmaster, operating until October, 1906. The settlement was noted for its lime kilns. In 2007 there was a canoe livery just west of the bridge on the north bank.

11.2 Barnaby Drain enters the river from the southwest.

9.3 Brown Drain enters the river from the north.

7.9 **Raisinville**. A man named Blanchard was the first settler at this point in 1823. In June of 1825 a post office opened called Raisinville. with Thomas B. Benjamin as the first postmaster. The post office operated until 1828. It is likely that the location of the post office changed with the residence of the postmaster. In 1832 the **West Raisinville** post office opened, operating until 1842. An 1870s map shows the **North Raisinville** post office at this point. To add to the directional confusion, as late as 1967 there was an **East Raisinville** church at the crossroads. The settlement was named for the river which bisects it.

7.75 Willow Run enters the river from the north.

7.8 Bridge. Raisinville Road crosses the river southwest-northeast. There was a wooden bridge built at this site as early as 1849, which was destroyed by an ice jam in 1887. It was not replaced for 80 years.

On the northeast corner of the bridge are a number of historic structures administered by the Monroe County Historical Society.

7.7 **Martha Barker Country Store Museum** The old Papermill School, at the junction of Raisinville Road and North Custer Drive, was named for the McDowell Papermill, which stood across the river when the school was built in the 1850s. The building operated as an active elementary school until

(Below) North Raisinville P.O. about half way between Dundee and Monroe on a map from the mid 1800s.

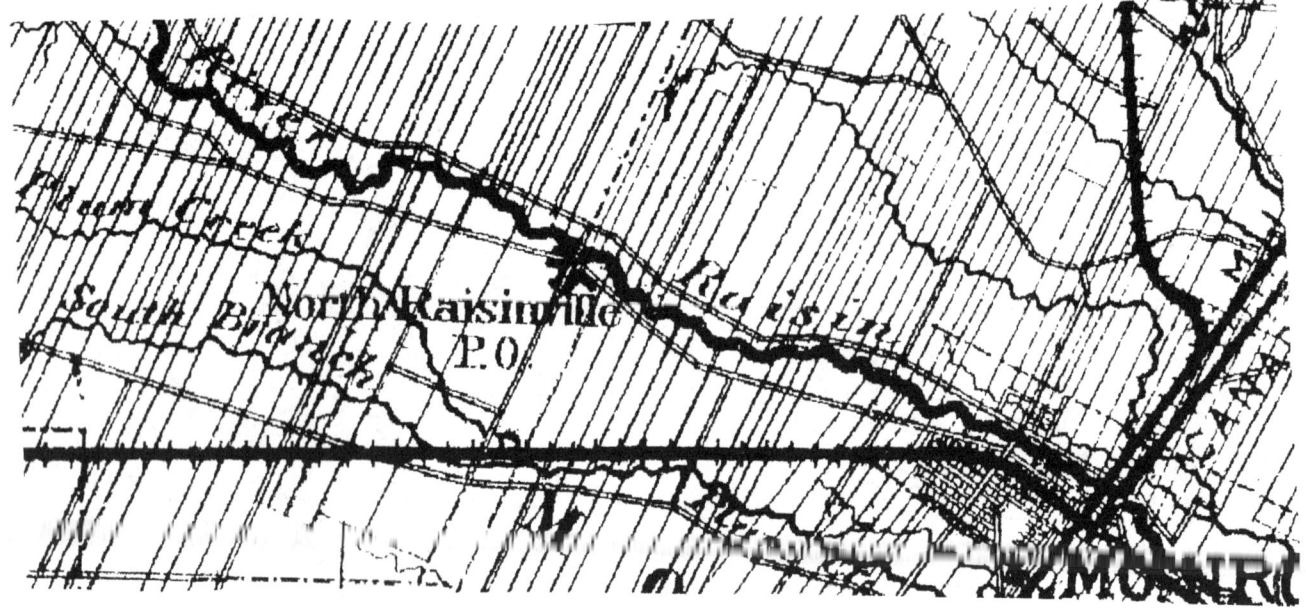

(Above) The Navarre-Anderson Trading Post, one of the oldest buildings in Michigan is part of an historic complex administered by the Monroe Historical Society.

1962. When it closed Martha Barker worked five years with a committee to turn the old school into a replica of a common country store about 1918. Artifacts were donated by local families and many items reflect the German background of the residents of that time. The building is open during Michigan Week in May and during the Monroe County Fair and other special occasions.

Navarre-Anderson Trading Post Complex. Just east of the old school stands an old trading post built by Francois M. (called Hutreau) Navarre in 1789, making it one of the oldest preserved structures in Michigan, and the oldest of French architecture and construction. It was used mainly to store grain and goods for trade until 1797 when it was converted into the Navaree family residence. In 1802 the building was sold to Colonel John Anderson, and then to Dr. Joseph Dazette, the first physician on the River Raisin, who was on friendly terms with the local Indians, which may have saved the building from destruction during the War of 1812. Colonel Anderson owned it again, 1816 to 1847, when it was sold to the Ilgenfritz family. When they decided to move it from its original location on Elm Street in Monroe, the historic nature of the structure was revealed. In 1972 land was donated at the present site and the building was moved there. To add to the site an old cabin was moved nearby to serve as the *cuisine d'ete*, a summer outdoor kitchen, which would have been used by the family living in the cabin. There is also a replica of a late 18th century French-Canadian barn, made with wooden pegs instead of nails. A number of pear trees on the grounds have been grafted from the descendents of trees which the French settlers brought to the area. The buildings are open at special times during the year, and the grounds, including many explanatory exhibits are open to visitors year round. Parking is available in front of the school.

7.7 McDowell Papermill. The south bank, just east of the Raisinville bridge was the site of the first papermill built on the Raisin. The manufacture of paper would become a major industry in the area. Monroe County was known for its newsprint and wrapping paper made from straw. This mill, first opened in 1838, was the first newsprint mill in the Midwest, and the first mill to produce straw paper commercially in the country.

7.7 At this point the river becomes the township boundary with Frenchtown Township, Monroe County, on the north bank, and Monroe Township, Monroe County on the south bank.

7.3-6.9 **Cranbrook Park** is a greenbelt which runs along the north bank of the river at Cranbrook subdivision. Also **St. Antoine's Park**, where the cross marks the site of an early Catholic cemetery.

7. Brest Drain enters the river from the north.

6.6 **Nevin Custer Home**. On the north side of the river, east of Bates Road, at what is now 3048 North Custer Drive, stands the farm which George Armstrong Custer and his brother, Nevin, along with their wives, purchased in 1871. Nevin, whose rheumatic heart kept him out of the army, was the only one of the Custer line to have children. General Custer's favorite horse, Dandy, was buried in the orchard near the barn. Visitors to this farm may have included Buffalo Bill Cody and Annie Oakley.

6.5 - 0 **Monroe**. By 1780 the best lands in the Detroit area had been taken and farmers, often in family groups, began to move into other river valleys in the southeast corner of the Lower Peninsula. Traditionally the first settler was Francois Navarre, who received a deed of land from the local Indians and built a trader's cabin in 1789 on what would be present-day Elm Street. By 1784 about a hundred French families, mostly from Canada, had settled on the north bank of the Raisin, reaching upriver nearly 15 miles inland. Called **Frenchtown** it became the third permanent settlement in what would later be Michigan, and, on November 21, 1815, only the second post office (after Detroit) with Laurent Durocher as the first postmaster. When A. B. Woodward became a judge on the court of Michigan Territory in 1805 he purchased 490 acres of land on the River Raisin at what would later be Monroe,

(Above) Waterloo Dam at Monroe from a 1908 postcard. The message on the back reads, "Went fishing Saturday and brought back 75 fish. Marie." (Bottom) A view photographed in 2008 with the lawn of Veterans Park in the foreground.

and proposed a settlement which he called **Euphemia.** Although he used his "cottage" (which he called, grandly, "Monticello") on the Raisin as a retreat, he sold the property in 1815, without making further commercial efforts. Frenchtown was nearly abandoned after the battle and massacre which occurred there during the War of 1812. In 1817 an American settlement was platted on the south bank of the river and named for newly elected President James Monroe. Monroe visited Michigan in 1817 and it was hoped that he might put in briefly at

ST. MARY'S ACADEMY, MONROE, MICH.

(Above) St. Mary's Academy along the banks of the Raisin at Monroe about 1912.

his namesake community. However, by the time the boat reached the western end of Lake Erie the seasick president continued directly on to Detroit. There had been much debate about whether the downtown area should be north or south of the river. Finally John Loranger who had bought the farm just west of the Francois Navarre home on the south bank, agreed to donate land to the new settlement for a courthouse, public square and roads. The post office was transferred from Frenchtown to the south bank and took the name of Monroe in 1824. Monroe was incorporated as a village in 1827 and as a city in 1837. The population in 2000 was 22,076 with a land area of 10.1 square miles. Old Frenchtown is now part of the City of Monroe, which has a very irregular boundary from just south of the airport, where it includes only the north bank communities until it crosses Telegraph Road. From that point east Monroe encompasses both banks of the river to Lake Erie along the government canal.

6.-5 **Patterson Gardens** A community on the south bank of the river, barely touching the riverbank, which shows on a 1967 survey map. Most of Patterson Gardens is now a part of Monroe.

5.5 **Waterloo Dam**, named for the former community of **Waterloo**, now part of Monroe. The dam is 12 feet tall and has a containment of 29 acres. Originally built of logs and heavy planking, the dam was rebuilt of concrete in 1904. It was the site of one of Michigan's earliest water-powered operations, the Waterloo Gristmill, built on the south bank in 1820.

5.5 - 5.3 **Veterans Park** on the north bank just below the dam is dedicated to the war dead of the county. A City of Monroe facility, it has a playground and picnic facilities and a large portion of the west end of the park contains veterans' memorials from various military engagements.

5.1 Bridge. U. S. 24, Telegraph Road, crosses the river near the west end of a small island mid river. **Mill Race Park** is nearby.

4.5 Railroad bridge. A bridge carries the C & O trains across the river north-south.

4.4 Bridge. Roessler Street crosses the river north-south.

4. 35 Small dam 1. To better control the water levels downtown several small dams were erected in the stream. The little dams also enhance fishing, but limit small boat traffic.

4.5 – 4 Site of St. Mary's Academy. In the fall of 1845 three young women began the Sisters, Servants of the Immaculate Heart of Mary, a Catholic women's order which now has a worldwide ministry. The following year they founded St.Mary's Academy, a Catholic school for girls, at this site, which grew to include post-high school classes and was certified as a four-year college in 1910. In 1927, the name was changed to Marygrove College and it was moved to Detroit. Although the original academy building was destroyed by fire, the grade and high school (which was mostly a boarding school) continued at Monroe, taught by the sisters whose convent and motherhouse was nearby. Faced with diminishing enrollments the grade school closed in 1970, and the boarding school in 1983. In 1988 the all-

The statue of George A. Custer now located on the north bank near the Monroe Street bridge.

girl high school was merged with Monroe Catholic Central High School, a formerly all-male school, to form the co-

(Below) The bridge about 1940.

ed establishment St. Mary Catholic Central High School. The large complex also includes a retirement residence, and the Raisin River Institute which states its mission as "to serve as a sustainable learning community dedicated to respect, nurture and promote the well-being of all creation."

4.3-4.1 **Sisters Island**, named for the occupants of the nearby convent.

4. Small dam 2.

A monument which marks the site of the battle in 1813

3.9 – 3.8 **St. Mary's Park** is located on the north bank of the river, west of Monroe Street.

3.9 Pedestrian Bridge.

3.8 Bridge. Monroe Street crosses the river north-south on a bridge constructed in 1990.

Just north of the bridge in the northwest corner of North Monroe and West Elm streets, stands a large equestrian statue "Sighting the Enemy" of local Civil War hero General George Armstrong Custer. As a child and young man he had attended school in Monroe, living with his married sister, and, in 1871 after his Civil War service, he and a brother purchased a farm nearby. The statue was designed by sculptor Edward C. Porter and erected by the State of Michigan in 1910. It first sat in the middle of the intersection near the courthouse south of the river, but in 1955 was moved to its present site. The image depicts Custer as a Civil War soldier at the time of the Battle of Gettysburg. After the Civil War he continued in military service and died in 1876 at the Battle of the Little Bighorn in the Black Hills.

3.8 – 3.65 **Altrusa Park**, a City of Monroe run downtown facility, on Front Street between Monroe and South Macomb streets.

3.7 Small Dam 3.

3.65 Bridge. Macomb Street on the **Veteran's Memorial Bridge** crosses the river north-south. Commemorative plaques are on the northwest and southeast corners.

(Above) Monroe's version of the triple bridges. Two railroad bridges and, at right, the vehicle bridge which carries Dixie Highway over the River Raisin.

3.64-3.1 **Soldiers and Sailors Park** runs along East Front Street on the south bank, between Wadsworth and Kentucky streets.

3.15 Small Dam 4.

3.1 Railroad bridge. Old Penn Central tracks cross to the factories on the south bank where it runs along Kentucky Street.

2.94 **Riviere aux Raisin Park**, a City of Monroe facility, on the northwest corner of the North Dixie Highway and East Elm Street. At present the park is undeveloped but contains a stone cairn erected in 1904 proclaiming:

> **Site of battles January 19-22, 1813**
> **Gen. Winchester in command and**
> **River Raisin massacre**
> **January 23, 1813**
> **Erected by the Civic Improvement**
> **Society**
> **of the Women of Monroe**

2.93 Bridge. M-50, North Dixie Highway, crosses southwest-northeast. Connects with Winchester Parkway.

2.96 Railroad bridge.

2.95 Railroad bridge. Formerly for the Detroit and Toledo Shore Line.

2.9 - 2.8 **Strong Island** shows at midstream on some maps. An earlier map calls it Nigger Island. It is no longer there and may have been removed during the building of the new Dixie Highway bridge.

2.5-2.3 **Sterling Island** near the south bank. Earlier this island was the site of the city docks. Now it is a park connected to the mainland by a footbridge. It bears the name of a former owner.

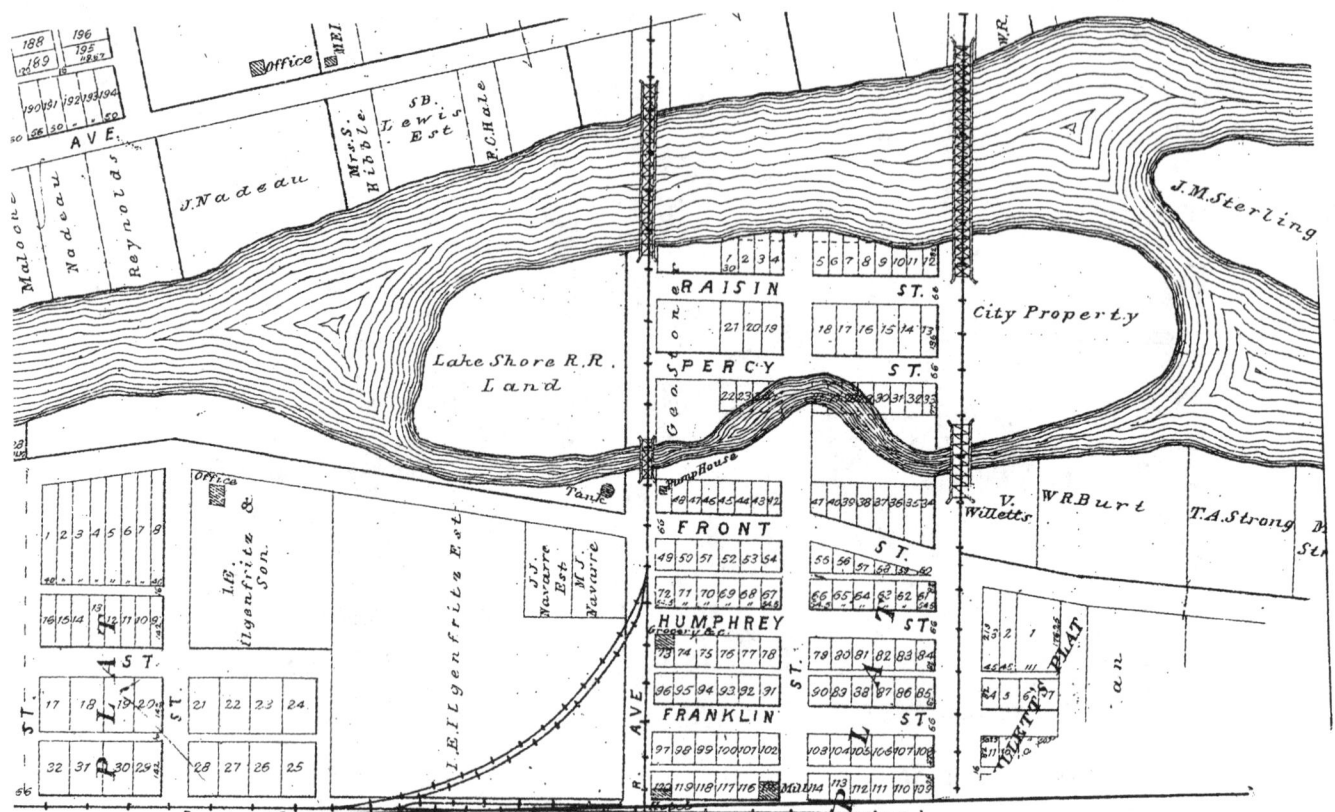

Islands come and go on the River Raisin. (Above) A map from about 1875 shows a large island in downtown Monroe with two railroad bridges crossing it and two city streets running parallel between them. (Below) In this 1929 Sanborn fire map there are three railroad tracks and a vehicular bridge with the same two streets, but the area is now connected to the mainland, the channel has been filled. (Inset in upper right of lower map) This 1967 survey map shows the same two islands near the "bump" but the name given the westernmost one is different.

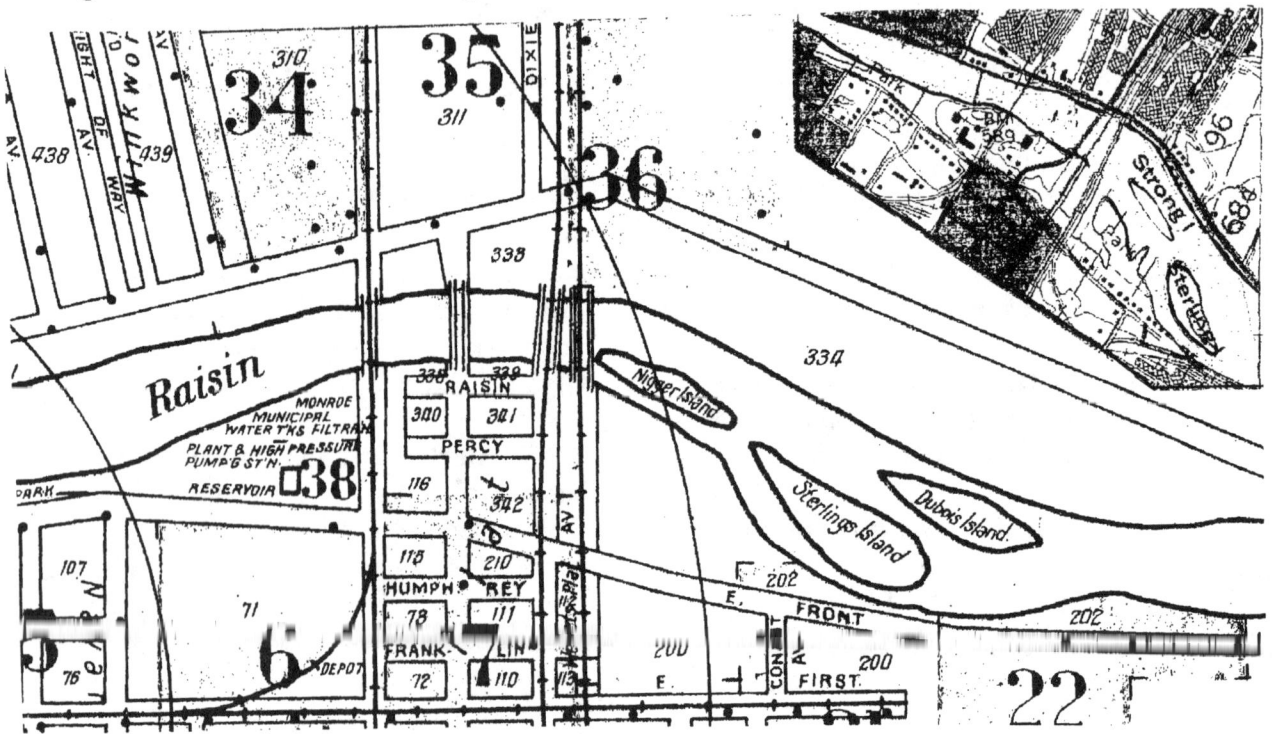

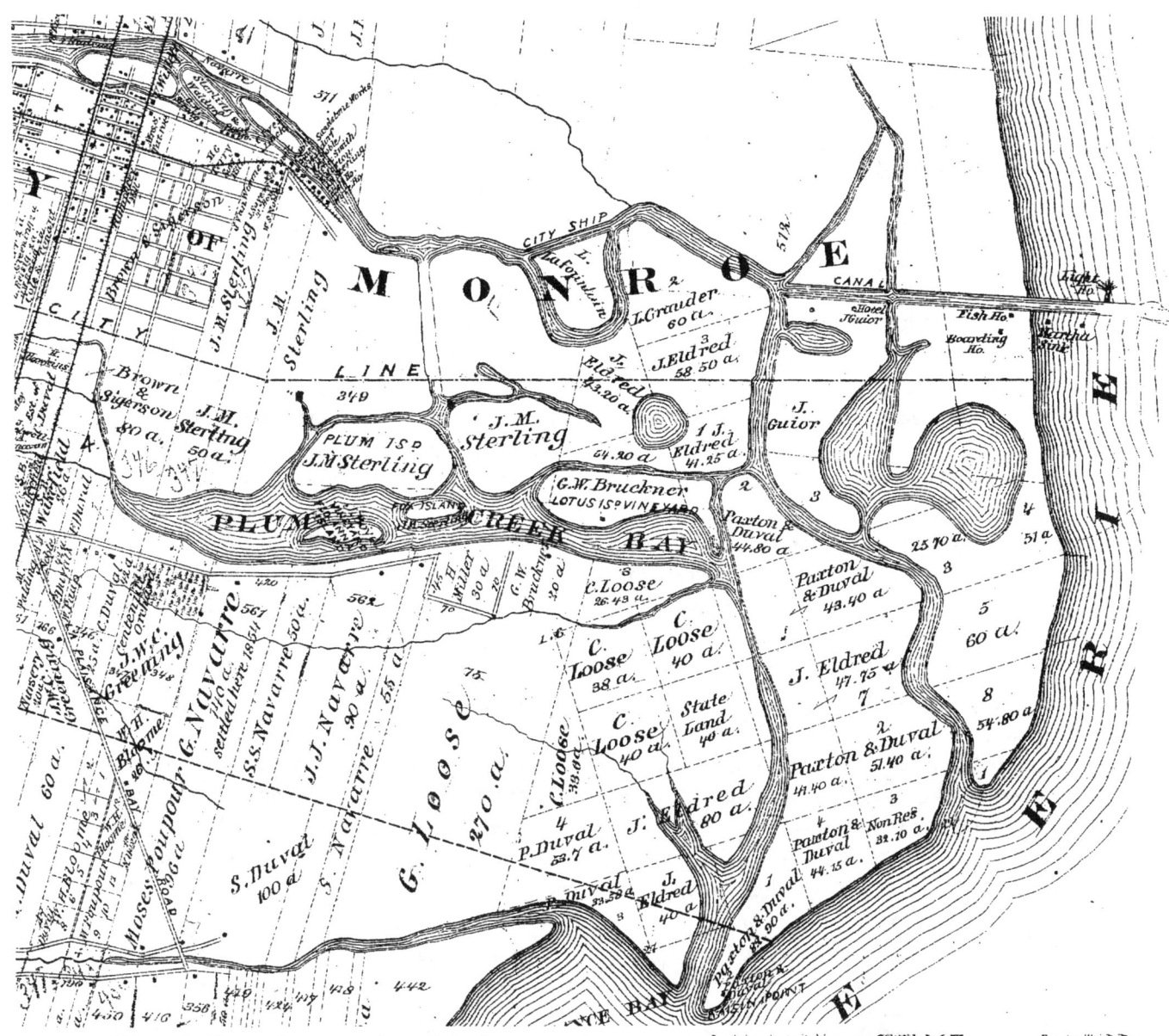

(Above) About the same time that the canal was creating a new mouth for the River Raisin in the 1830s another short canal, in the center of the map with the words "City Ship," was cutting off a deep turn to create a new island. In 1932, seeking a wide spot in the river for large boats to turn around, the island was removed. *(Right)* The turning basin has 19-21 feet of water on this 1967 survey map. On the old map above note the former river channel which exited at La Plaisance Bay at Raisin Point. Much of the area between the city and Lake Erie is marshland, with streams, open water and islands.

2.4 **Hellenberg Boat Launch** on the south bank, parking area with a foot bridge to Sterling Island.

2. Bridge. Interstate-75 crosses the river southwest-northeast.

1.5 - 1.3 Turning basin on south side of the channel. Part of the improvements made in the River Raisin beginning in 1838 was the straightening of an oxbow at this point, a shortcut that old maps refer to as the "City Ship Canal." This left a triangular island in the middle. After industry came to the mouth of the river in the 1930s, a space was needed in the river itself large enough and deep enough for Lakes boats to turn around. The island was removed leaving a turning basin which a 1967 survey map notes is 18 to 21 feet deep. According to Port of Monroe records approximately 15 large Lakes boats a year take advantage of the turning basin.

1.3 - 1 Factory, on the north bank. In 1927 the old Hotel Lotus, near the piers was razed to make way for the Newton Steel Company plant, a facility made famous by a strike in the 1930s. The site was later taken over by the Ford Stamping Plant. The facilities, most recently used by Automotive Components, were scheduled to close in 2008

.8 A small spur of water goes off to the south marking the old bed of the River Raisin which turned south at this point and mingled with Plum Creek, before exiting into La Plaisance Bay at Raisin Point to the south. The channel into Lake Erie from this point westward today is a canal finished in 1842, designed to be 100 feet wide and 10 feet deep. Later the river, up to the turning basin, was dredged to 21 feet in depth.

One of the sights that brought visitors during the early 20th Century was the American Lotus *(Nelumbo hitea)* which grew in swampy profusion near the river mouth. Development near the mouth and flooding in the 1950s nearly obliterated

(Below) An old engraving of the construction of the City Ship Canal, opened for use in 1842.

DREDGE USED IN CONSTRUCTING CITY CANAL AT MONROE

![Monroe Pier, Mich. View on Government Canal.]

(Above) A lone boat sails into the Government Canal at Monroe, from a 1908 postcard.

the annual show. However cleanup efforts in the 21st Century and lower water levels on Lake Erie are bringing about a return of the lotus. They bloom at mid-summer and can be seen from land along East Dunbar Road and on La Plaisance Bay near Raisin Point. The lotus is now a protected flower and should not be picked.

.5 On the south bank there is a small parking lot for a fishing access site, just inland from the power plant. Cars may be parked on the north side of the access road. From April to the end of October fishermen on foot may cross the street, and enter behind a chain link fence to a trail that runs south along the canal. Fishing is from the wooden piers only.

.7 - .3 Power plant, a coal-fired plant on the south bank, built by the Detroit Edison Company in 1966, is now owned by DTE Energy. It is one of the largest coal-fired plants in the world. Although built right at the harbor entrance, planners stated that delivery of coal by water was not anticipated. However, since about 2000 a portion of the coal needed for operation has been delivered by Lakes bulk carriers. The coal is unloaded at the Edison docks right at the mouth of the river, and the coal boats are able to back into Lake Erie without coming into the river to turn at the turning basin.

.1- 0 After the canal to Lake Erie was finished in 1842 a beacon light was planned for the north pier as Monroe harbor was then the only artificial harbor in Michigan on Lake Erie. It was approved by Congress in 1848, but not completed until the following year. An octagonal wooden tower showed a fixed red light. The keeper's house was constructed on land, but in 1859 it was moved out on the pier itself. The pier was rebuilt in 1885 along with a new one and a half story keeper's house that incorporated the lighthouse structure with the tower protruding from the center of the roof. In 1900 it had a 4th-order Fresnel lens having a 13-mile visibility. It was replaced in 1916 by an automated gas light which was installed on a skeletal steel tower beside the lighthouse on the pier. The lighthouse structure was sold in 1922, dismantled and removed. Today there are only Coast Guard lights at the river entrance although the twin 816 foot stacks of the Edison power plant, with both red and white lights at night, help boats on the lake locate the harbor and the yard lights at the facility help illuminate the entrance.

.0 Enter Lake Erie at an indentation on the coast called Brest Bay, protected on the north by the projection of Stony Point. The approximate mean lake elevation of Lake Erie is 572 feet above sea level.

(Below) The Monroe lighthouse about 1912.

Bibliography

Angus, Esther T. Wolfe *What's Past is Prologue: Swainsville andBrooklyn, 1832 – 1914)* (Exponent Press: Brooklyn) n.d.

Battle and Massacre of the River Raisin (Battle of French Town) excerpts from the *Niles Weekly Register*, Baltimore, February 13, 1813; March 6, 1813; April 10, 1813. (Compiled by Wilma B. Price for the Monroe County Historical Society and the Monroe County Library System) 1981.

Bidlack, Russell E. *The Yankee Meets the Frenchman: River Raisin, 1817-1830, Social – Political – Military* (Historical Society of Michigan: Lansing) 1965.

Blois, John T *Gazetteer of the State of Michigan* (Sydney L. Rood & Co.: Detroit) 1838.

Bonner, Richard Illenden, ed. *Memoirs of Lenawee County, Michigan* (Western Historical Association: Madison, Wisconsin) 1909

Clark, Thomas "Address to the Pioneer Society of Lenawee County, June 10, 1878. *MPHC* Vol 11, p. 423-424.

Clift, G. Glenn *Remember the Raisin!* (Kentucky Historical Society: Frankfort, Kentucky) 1961.

Coffin, William F. *1812: The War and its Moral: A Canadian Chronicle* (John Lovell: Montreal) 1864.

Dudley, Thomas P. "Battle and Massacre at Frenchtown, Michigan, January, 1813" *MPHC* Vol. 22, p. 436-443.

Dundee Area Sesquicentennial, 1824-1974 (Dundee Area Sesquicentennial Committee)

Greene, Marian Palmer *Reflections in the River Raisin* n.p., n.d.

Hamil, Fred C. *Michigan in the War of 1812* (Michigan Historical Commission: Lansing) 1960.

Hatcher, Harlan *Lake Erie* (The Bobbs-Merrill Company: Indianapolis) 1945.

Hinsdale, Wilbert B. *Archeological Atlas of Michigan* (University of Michigan Press: Ann Arbor) 1931.

History of Hillsdale County, Michigan (Everts & Abbott: Philadelphia) 1879.

History of Jackson County, Michigan (Interstate Publishing Co.: Chicago) 1881.

History of the Great Lakes, Illustrated (J. H. Beers & Co.: Chicago) 1899.

History of Washtenaw County, Michigan (Chas. C. Chapman & Co.: Chicago) 1881.

Hogaboam, James J. *The Bean Creek Valley. Incidents of its Early Settlement.* (Jas. M Scarritt,, Publisher: Hudson, Mich.) 1876.

Hutchinson, Craig E. and Kimberly A. *Monroe: The Early Years* (Arcadia: Charleston, South Carolina) 2004.

Karpinski, Louis C. *Historical Atlas of Great Lakes and Michigan* (Michigan Historical Commission: Lansing) 1931.

Lane, Kit *Ohio vs Michigan: Guns Across the Maumee* (Pavilion Press: Douglas, Michigan) 2001.

Larson, John W. *Essayons: A History of the Detroit District U. S. Army Corps of Engineers* (U. S. Army Corps of Engineers, Detroit Distrtict) 1981.

Lindquist, Charles *Adrian: The City that Worked* (Lenawee County Historical Society: Adrian) 2004.

Lindquist, Charles *The Anti-Slavery Underground Railroad Movement in Lenawee County, Michigan, 1830-1860* (Lenawee County Historical Society: Adrian) 1999.

Lindquist, Charles *Lenawee Reflections* (Lenawee County Historical Society: Adrian) 1992.

Lindquist, Charles *Spanning the Years: A History of Blissfield, Michigan, 1824-1999* (Lenawee County Historical Society: Adrian) 2000.

Lund, Harry C. *Michigan Wildflowers* (Altwerger & Mandel Publishing Co.: West Bloomfield) 1991.

Macleod, David I. ed., *Mapping in Michigan & the Great Lakes Region* (Michigan State University Press: East Lansing) 2007.

Meints, Graydon M. *Michigan Railroads and Railroad Companies* (Michigan State University Press: East Lansing) 1992.

Michigan and Its Resources (Robert Smith & Co,, State Printers) 1893.

Miller, James Martin *The Amazing Story of Henry Ford* (James C. Bailey & Company: Chicago) 1922.

Miller, Raymond C. *Kilowatts at Work: A History of the Detroit Edison Company* (Wayne State University Press: Detroit) 1957.

Miller, Raymond C. *The Force of Energy: A Business History of the Detroit Edison Company* (Michigan State University Press) 1971.

Naveaux, Ralph and Shana Gruber *A Brief History of the City and County of Monroe, Michigan, 1830-1930* (Monroe County Historical Museum) 2001.

Old Manchester Village (Prepared for the Village of Manchester by Ann Arbor Federal Savings) 1974.

Palmer, Jane *History of Manchester, Michigan* (n.p., n.d.)

"Post-Remediation Sediment Sampling on the Raisin River Near Monroe, Michigan" (U. S. Environmental Protection Agency) 2002.

Schneider, Marie A. *Manchester's First Hundred Years, 1867-1967* (Manchester Centennial Committee: Manchester) 1967

Segal, Howard P. *Recasting the Machine Age: Henry Ford's Village Industries* (University of Massachusetts Press: Amherst, 2005.

Towns, Gary L. *A Fisheries Survey of the River Raisin, August 1984* (Fisheries Division, Michigan Department of Natural Resources: Lansing) 1985,

Waldron, Clara *One Hundred Years A Country Town: The Village of Tecumseh, Michigan, 1824-1924* (Thomas A. Riordan, publisher: n.p.) 1968.

Whitney, W. A. and R. I. Bonner *History and Biographical Record of Lenawee County, Michigan* (W. Stearns & Co., Printers: Adrian) 1879.

Wildflowers of Michigan (Michigan Department of Conservation and Federated Garden Clubs of Michigan) [1940?]

Wing, Talcott E. "Continuation of the History of Monroe" *MPHC* Vol. 16, p. 374-382.

Wing, Talcott E "History of Monroe County, Michigan" *MPHC* Vol. 4, p. 318-324.

Woodford, Frank B. *Mr. Jefferson's Disciple: A Life of Justice Woodward* (Michigan State: East Lansing) 1953.

MPHC – *Michigan Pioneer and Historical Collection*

Index

Academy Road 74
Adrian 2,5,43,69,73-73
Adrian Street 78
Adrian Township 73
Allen Road 67
Allen, John 26,30
Alley, Elias 53
Altrusa Park 94
American Lotus 47-48.
  47,98-99,99
American Revolution 19
Amherstburg, Canada 28
Anderson, John 20,28,89,
  90
Ann Arbor 5
Ann Arbor RR 85
Atkinson, Hannah W. 88
Atlas Mill Dam 67,68
Austin Road 62,65,66
Austin, Harvey 62
Automotive Components
  98
Automotive Products 61

Bachmayer, Clara 78
Bachmayer, Joseph 78
Baldwin, Horatio N. 68
Ballard, Bland W. 30
Barker, Martha 89
Barnaby Drain 88
Bay Drain 75
Bear Creek 75
Bear River 6
Beaver Creek 73
Beck, Edward 34
Benjamin, Thomas B. 88
Benton Harbor 15,52
Bethel Church Road 64
Black Creek 75
Blanchard, Stillman 70
Bliss, Aaron T. 32
Bliss, Hervey 22,77
Blissfield 5,7,22,35,37,44,
  74,76,77,78,79,89,77-79
Blissfield Junction 74
Blissfield Township 75,77
Blois, John T. 5
boatbuilding 10-11
Bolles Harbor Boat Club
  48
Bradish, John B. 9

Bradish, Joseph 9,10
Brenott Drain 79
Brest Bay 43,100
Brest Drain 90
Bridge School 87,87
Bridgewater Township 66
Brooklyn 22,37,38,52,
  52,56,60,60,61,61
Brooklyn Road 56
Brooklyn, NY 61
Brown Drain 88
Brown, Joseph W. 21,69,
  73
Brown, Solomon 66
Brownstown 8,8,25,29
Brownsville (or Brown-
  ville) 16,17, 68,69
Bruckner Bridge 87
Brule, Etienne 13
Bucholtz Road 80
Buffalo 10
Burnett, B.F. 33
Burt Street 70
Burton and White Drain
  81
Bush, George W. 41

C & O RR 92
Cadillac, Antoine de la
  Mothe 19
Cambridge Junction 21,21,
  22,52,59
Cambridge Junction State
  Historic Park 22,57
Cambridge Township 57
Camp Drain 79
Campeau, Alexis 18
Canada 25
*Canada ou de la Nouvelle
  France* 6
Carey and Warner 8
Cary Road 55
Case & Davis distillery 65
Cass, Lewis 19,61
Catholic Central High
  School 93
Cement 55
Cement City 52,55
Chandler, Elizabeth
  Margaret 16
Chase Road 72

Chase's Station 72,72
Chicago & Southern
  Canada Rwy. 85
Chicago 22,23,53
Chicago Boulevard 72
Chicago Highway 70
Chippawa 12
Chippewa 13
City of Buffalo 10-11,*11*
City Ship Canal 98,99
Civic Improvement Assn.
  95
Clara Backmayer Park 78
Clark Lake 52,53,56,56
Clark, Calvin 85
Clark, Thaddeus 22,68
Clayton 73
Clemente Drain 75
Cleveland and Buffalo
  Transit Co. 11
Cleveland Lake 57
Cleveland, Ohio 44
Clinton 5,22,65,67,
  67,68,68
Clinton Township 67
Clinton Woolen Mill 67,67
Clinton, DeWitt 68
Cody, Buffalo Bill 90
Cole, Thomas G. 21,82
Columbia 53,56
Columbia Township 52,
  55,58
Comfort Road 72
Comstock, Addison 73,74
Comstock, Darius 16,73
Consumers Power 37,70,
  79
Cooley Road 57
Cranbrook Park 90
Cranbrook Subdivision 90
Crockett Road 75
Curtis, Alonzo 85
Custer Drive 84,88
Custer Road 88
Custer, George Armstrong
  31,90,94,95
Custer, Nevin 90
Cuyahoga River 44

D H & I RR 34
dams 37-40

Index

Dandy 90
Dayton, Ohio 25
Dazette, Joseph 89
de Brebeuf, Jean 13
de Casson, Dollier 13
de la Salle, Robert 13
de Vaugondy, Robert 6
Deane, Isaac 74
Dearborn 37
Dearborn, Henry 12,20,87,
Deerfield 3,10,22,77,79, *80*,80,82
Deerfield Road 75,82
Deerfield Township 79
DeLamatter, Anson H. 56
DeLamatter, DeWitt C. 56
DeLisle 6
Detroit & Toledo Shore Line 95
Detroit 9,10,11,13,19,20, 22,23,24,25,*25*,29,40, 43,73,90,92,93
Detroit Edison Co.11,37, 40-41,*41*,45,99,100
Detroit, Monroe & Toledo Shortline 43
Detroit, Toledo & Ironton RR 85
Dewey, Francis 16-17
Dixie Highway 32,95
Dorr, Couch C. 64
DTE Energy 41.99
Dunbar Road 99
Duncan Street 65
Dundee 5,10,15,21,35, 37,40,45,*77*,83-84,*83*, *84*,88
Dundee Cement Co. 85
Dundee Hydraulic Power Co. 37
Dundee Township 82
Dundee, Scotland 83
Dunlap Drain 82
Durocher, Laurent 90
Duvall, Frank 34
Duvall, Wilmer 34

East Raisinville 88
Edmondon, John M. 30
Elliot, William 28
Ellis Park 77-78

Ellis, A.D. 77
Ellis, Edward D. 20
Elm Street 24,32,34, 90,94,95
Embargo Act 23
Erie and Kalamazoo RR 7,74
Erie Canal 68
Euphemia 91
Evans Creek *65*,69,*70*,72
Evans, Musgrove 21,69,73
Exchange Place 65

Fargo, James Harvey 22, 65
Fargo, Steven 22
Feather, John 64
firewater 16
Fish Consumption Advisory 44
fishing 44,45,99
Flat Rock 37
floods 33-36
Floodwood Creek 10,*77*, 79
Floyd C.Tate Memorial Park 68
Ford Motor Co. 11,61,65, 84
Ford Stamping Plant 98
Ford, Henry 37-38,40,54
Fort Dearborn 23
Fort Defiance 25
Fort Malden 25,*25*,28,29
Fort Meigs 29
Fort Wayne 23,24,
Fort Wayne, Ind.15,25,*25*
Frankfort, Ky. 29
Franklin County, Kentucky 25
French and Indian War 19
French land claims 85-86, *86*
French settlers 9,12,19,20
Frenchtown 8,*8*,10.15, 20,23,???29,75,90-91
Frenchtown Township 90
Front Street 34,95
Furnace Street 65

Galinee, Father 13

Galloway, Stephen 72
Gambleville 53
Gazetteer of Michigan 5
Georgian Bay 13
Gilbert, Harry H. 65
Gilbert, John 22
Gilbert, Joseph O. 64
Giles, George 77,78
Gilett, Amasa 33
Gleason Brook 75
Globe Milling Co. 70
Goff, Timothy B. 22,75
Goose Creek 52,52,53, *53*,*61*,61
Goose Lake *52*,55
Government Canal 2
Grand River 5,14,15,33, 52,56
Grape 10,37,*83*,87,*87*-88
Grass Lake 52
Graves, Benjamin F. 30
Great Black Swamp 77
Green Bay 13
Griffin 13,*13*
Grosvenor 75

Hahn Drain 75
Hamlin 10,*85*,85
Hamlin, Hannibal 85
Harkness Drain 73
Harrison Drain 73
Harrison, William Henry 30
Hart, Nathaniel F. S. 30
Hawley, Chauncey 61
Hayden Mills 38,*39*,40, 70,*72*
Hazelbank 16
Hazen Creek 73
Heights, The *60*,60
Hellenberg Boat Launch 48,98
Hennepin, Louis 13
Hickman, Paschal 30
Hinsdale, Wilbert 14,17
Hotel Lotus 43,98
Hudson Township 73
Hull, William 23,24,27
Hunt, William 22,62
Huron River 5,14,15,36,37

Index

Ilgenfritz family 90
Illinois River 15
Indian Crossing Park 72
Indian reservation 15
Indians 9,16
Industrial Automotive Products 40
Ingersoll, Riley 21,83
Irish Hills 52,60
Iron Creek *65*,67
Iroquois 13,15
Island Park (Adrian) 74

Jackson 5,22
Jackson County 5,63
Jackson Gear 40,61
Jackson Road 54
Jefferson 53,*53*,55,56,*56*
Jefferson Road 56
Jefferson, Thomas 20,56
Jennings, Arthur 36
Jerome, Charles 19
Jerome, John Baptiste 19
Johnson, Lyndon B. 40
Johnson, Oliver 20
Johnson, Richard Mentor 30
Jolliet, Adrien 13
Jolliet, Louis 13
Jouett, C. 12,20

Kalamazoo River 5,8,14
Kankakee River 15
Kedzie, William 21-22, 77,80
Kedzie's Grove 22,80
Kellar Drain 79
Kelly's Corners *53*,56
Kentucky Street 95
Kingsley, J. H. 37
Krusty, F. 18

La Plaisance Bay 6,7,*7*,13, 22,40,48,97,98,99
La Plaisance Road 34,70
Labady, Piere 18
Laberdee Road 73,74
Lake Columbia *52*,55,56
Lake Erie 5,6,7,*7*,11,13, 22,40,41,42,43,44,46, 47,52,75,92,97,98,99, 100
Lake Erie Center 36
Lake Huron 13
Lake LeAnn 54
Lake Michigan 8,14,15, 52,56
Lake Ontario 13
Lake Shore & Michigan Southern RR 21,63,68, 72,75,78
Lake Somerset *53*,53,55
Lake Somerset Property Owners Assn. 54
Lanserainte, Jean Baptiste 18
Lansing 33
le Carron, Joseph 13
Lebanon, Ohio 25
Lenawee County 5,8
Lenawee Junction *74*,74, 75
LeRoy *73*,74
Lewis, William 25
lighthouse 2,100,*100*
Little Goose Lake 55
Little Raisin Creek 82
Little St. Joseph River 15
Little Stony Lake 58
Loranger, John 92
Love, Israel 61
Lyon (or Lyons) *78*,78
Lyons (Ohio) 5

Mackinac Island 19.23
Macomb Street 94
Macon 16
Macon Creek *15*,*83*,85
Madison, George 27-28,29
Main Street 65
Manchester 5,22,33,35, 37,40,*61*,65,66,*65*,*66*
Manchester Enterprise 33
Manchester Milling Co. 22,65
Manchester Township 63
Manchester Township, NY 65
Maple Grove Cemetery 82
Marquette, Jacques 13
Marshall 8
Martha Barker Country Store Museum 88
Marygrove College 93
Mason Run 5
Maumee River 5,6,8,*8*,15, 25,*25*,26,29
Maumee Street Bridge 74
McCloskey, James 15
McCourtie Park 54,*54*
McCourtie, W. H. L. 54
McCracken, Virgil 30
McDowell Papermill 88, 90
McMillan Canal 45
McNeill, Helen L. 68
Meade, James 30
Mercer Road 53,*53*
Mercury Lake *52*,57,57
Michigan Department of Natural Resources 22,44
Michigan International Speedway 57,*57*
Michigan Territory 6
Michigan Volksfreund 18
Michigan Water Resources Commission 44
Milan 85
Mill Highway 72
Mill Race Park 92
Mill Road 63
Mill Street 61,*61*
Miller Drain 81
Milwaukee Road 69
Mississippi River 13
Monroe 2,5,6,10,11,20-21, 37,42,48,52,82,*83*,88,90-100,*91-100*
Monroe Avenue 31
Monroe Boat Club 48
Monroe city docks 10
Monroe Civic Improvement Society 31
Monroe County 5
Monroe County Fair 89
Monroe County Historical Society 88,89
Monroe Equipment Co. 11
Monroe marshes 48
Monroe Pike Road 58
Monroe Record-Commercial 34
Monroe Street 24,94

Index

Monroe Township 90
Monroe Yacht Club 2, 42, 43, 48
Monroe, James 20, 91
Montgomery, John H. 85
Monticello 91
Montreal 13
Moon Lake *52*
Morse, Moses 20
mounds 16-17, *17*, 70
Mud Creek 9
Mud Lake 52
Murciak Dam 87, *87*

Nankin Mills 37
Nanticoke Generating Station 41
Napoleon 23
National Battlefield 32
Navarre, Francois 19, 24, 26, 90, 92
Navarre, Francois M. (Hutreau) 89
Navarre-Anderson Trading Post 89
navigation 10-11
Nelumbo hitea 47, *47*-48, 98
Nevin Custer Home 90
New York Central RR 65
Newburg 68, *68*
Newburg Highway 68
Newburgh 37
Newport, Kentucky 25
Newton Steel Co. 43, 98
Niagara 29
Niagara River 13
Nigger Island 95
Nooney Dam *60*, 60
North Raisinville *88*, 88
Northern Indiana 10
Northville 37
Northwest Ordinance 8
Norvell 22, *61*
Norvell Lake 62
Norvell Township 62
Norvell, John 63
Norvell-Manchester Drain 63
Norvill township 52
Nummasepee 6

Oakley, Annie 90
Oakwood Beach 60
Ogden Township 74, 75
Ohio 5, 6, 8, 20
Ohio River 25
Old Sauk Trail 22
Onemile Lake *52*, *57*, 57
Onsted State Wildlife Management Area. 57
Ottawa 12, 13, 15
Otter Creek 5, 12, 34

Palmyra 3, 5, *74*, 75
Palmyra Township 74
Palmyra, N. Y. 9, 75
Papermill School 88
Parks Corners *64*
Pattawatamy 12
Patterson Gardens 92
PCBs 44, 45, 46, 47
Pearl Street 77
Penn Central RR 73, 74, 82
Peters, Richard 21, 81-82
Petersburg 21, *35*, *77*, 77, *81*, 81-82
Petersburg Road 82
Petersburgh 5
Phelps Lake 58, *60*
Phoenix 37
Pickeral Lake *52*, *57*. 57
Pierce Road 63
piers 6, 42, 100
Piquot, Ohio 25
Plant Bowen 41
Pleasant Lake Road 64
Pleasant Valley 73
Plum Creek 5, 98
Plum Creek Bay 45
Plum Creek Wildlife Area 45
Plymouth 37
portages 14-15, *14*
Porter, Edward C. 94
Pottawatomi 13, 15, 16
power production 37-41
Proctor, Henry A. 27, 30
Pulier, Joseph 19
Purple Gang 54

Quigley, Charles 36

Raisin Basin 66-67, *67*
Raisin Center 10, 72, *72*
Raisin Center Highway 72
Raisin PO 10
Raisin Point 48, 97, 98, 99
Raisin River Institute 94
Raisin River PO 10
Raisin Township 72
Raisin Valley Land Trust 46
Raisine River 8, *8*
Raisinville 10, 88
Raisinville Road 88
Raisinville Station *85*, 85
Raisinville Township 85, *86*, 86, 87
Raison River 8, *8*
Red Millpond 69, *70*, 71
"Remember the Raisin!" 30
Remington, William 83
Richfield 64
Ripley's Believe it or Not! 3, 5
River Raisin (town) 65, 66-67, *67*
River Raisin & Lake Erie RR 7
River Raisin Battlefield Center 32
River Raisin Festival 77
River Raisin PO 10
River Raisin Watershed Council 46, 48
River Rouge 37
Riviere aux Ours 6, *75*, 75
Riviere aux Raisin Park 32, 95
Riviere aux Raisins 8, 19
Roe Drain 82
Roessler Street 93
Round Lake Highway 57
Russel Drain 81
Russell Road 72

Saline 85
Saline River 14, 15, 36, *83*, 85
Sand Creek (Madison Twp.) 73
Sand Hill Road 53, *53*

Index

Sandy Creek 5
Saugatuck 14,52
Schneider, Louis 70
Sharon *64*,64
Sharon Hollow 64
Sharon Hollow Road 64
Sharon Mills *39*,40,*61*, *63*,63-64
Sharon Plain 64
Sharon Township 33,63
Sharon Valley Road 63,64
Sharon, Conn. 64
Sharonville 40,64
Sharonville State Wildlife Management 52,63
Ship canal 7
"Sighting the Enemy" 94, *95*
Simpson, John 30
Sisters Island 94
Sisters, Servants of the Immaculate Heart of Mary 93
Slager Road 79
Smith, George U. 70
Soldiers and Sailors Park 95
Somerset 53,*53*,54
Somerset Center *52*,*53*,53, 54
Somerset Township 53
Somerset, NY 53
Soules, James 65
Soulesville 65
South Branch River Raisin *69*,73-74
South Lake *52*,*57*,57
Southern Michigan 10
St. Antoine's Park 90
St. Joseph 15
St. Joseph of the Maumee 15,52
St. Joseph River 52
St. Lawrence Seaway 11, 48
St. Mary's Catholic Central High School 94
St. Mary's Park 94
St. Mary's Academy *92*,93
St. Mary's River 25
Stacy Drain 82

Staib Road 68
Standish Pond *70*,70,72
Sterling Island 95,98
Sterling State Park 43,45
Sterling, Joseph M. 10
Stetson, Turner 69
Stoney Point 28,100
Stony Creek 73
Strong Island 95
Sturgeon, River of 6
Summerfield 81
Summerfield Township 80
Sunset Beach *60*,60
Sutton Road 72
Suzor, Marie 24
Swaine, Calvin H. 22,61
Swainesville 22,61
Sweeney Lake 52,63
Sweezey Lake 63
Swezzey Lake 52,63

Taylor Road 55
Tecumseh (Chief) 28,30, 69
Tecumseh 5,16,17,21,*36*, *37*,*38*,*39*,40,65,*68*,*69*,69- 72,*72*,73
Tecumseh Highway 70
Tecumseh Township 69
Telegraph Road 92
Terrill, John 22,68
Thames River *25*,29-30
Tiffany, Alexander R. 75
Todd, John 28
Toledo & Western RR 78
Toledo 6,10,25,52,74
toll bridge 85
Trabajo Rustico 54
Treaty of Paris 19
Treaty of Ghent 19,23
turning basin *97*,98,99

U.S. Environmental Protection Agency 45
University of Toledo 36

Valley Road 73
Van Akin, Simeon 31
Van Ness, S. 83
Van Ness's Mills 83
Ventura Road 58

Veteran's Memorial Bridge 94
Veterans Park 91
Vicary Road 55
Vineyard Lake 22,*52*,60

Wabash River 15
Wadsworth Street 95
Waldron Road 53
Walker Brook 75
Walker Tavern 21,*21*,22
Walker Tavern Complex 57
Walker, Sylvester S. 21, 22,57
Wallace Road 66
Wampler Lake Road 60
War of 1812 23-32
Washtenaw County 5
Washtenaw County Parks 39,40,64
Water Wheel Community 67
Waterloo 92
Waterloo Dam *91*,92
Waterloo Gristmill 92
Wayne, Anthony 24
West Raisinville 10,88
Wheatland Township 5
Wilder Road 66,67
Wiley Drain 79
Willow Run 88
Wilmoth Road 73
Winchester Parkway 95
Winchester, James 24,25,26,27,32,95
Winfield 85
Wing, Austin E. 21,69,82
Wing, Talcott 30
Wolf Creek 43
Wolf Lake Road 62
Wolverine Manufacturing and Fabricating Co. 40,84
Woodstock *53*,55
Woodstock Township 54, 57
Woodward, A. B. 90-91
Worck, Rudolph 18
Wyandotte 13
Young, John H. 8
Ypsilanti 37

Credits and Acknowledgements

p. 8 (bottom) From a *Map of the United States Exhibiting Its Principal, Canals & Railroads Engraved to Accompany Baldwin's Universal Pronouncing Gazetteer.* Engraved by J. H. Young.

p. 9 Letter from Joseph Bradish to John B.Bradish, February 7, 1819, Bentley Historical Library, University of Michigan, Ann Arbor, Michigan.

p. 14, 17 Based on *Archeological Atlas of Michigan,* by Wilbert B. Hinsdale (University of Michigan Press: Ann Arbor) 1931.

p. 24 Drawing of Navarre cabin by artist Ann Gray, Ganges Township, Allegan County, 2008.

p. 41, 97 Map based on a 2004 navigational chart for the West End of Lake Erie published by the National Oceanic and Atmospheric Administration, U. S. Department of Commerce.

p. 44 Fish Consumption Advisory is a summary of guidelines issued by the State of Michigan in 2007.

p.45 Fish drawings from *Great Lakes Nature Guide* published by the Michigan United Conservation Clubs about 1974.

p.81, 84, 86, 87, 88, 96, 97 (top) Maps, some undated, from the former Monroe office of TransAmerica Title Company.

p. 100 Drawing of the old Monroe lighthouse from several vintage photographs by artist Ann Gray, Ganges Township, Allegan County, 2008.

Other illustrations include old postcards or maps taken from the collection of the author, photographs taken by the author, and maps created specifically for this volume.

The author would like to recognize the assistance of many people along the course of the River Raisin including the staffs of the libraries in Blissfield, Clinton and Monroe, the Old Mill Museum at Dundee, the Monroe County Historical Museum at Monroe, the Cambridge Junction Historical State Park, the River Raisin Watershed Council, River Raisin Battlefield Visitor Center, and the office of the Port of Monroe. Also C. Patrick Labadie of NOAA and Jim Woodruff for his assistance with the entire Rivers of Michigan Series.

Rivers of Michigan Series

The Kalamazoo

The Kalamazoo River of southern Michigan rises in the Irish Hills south of Jackson in Hillsdale County and flows gently westward for about 200 miles until it exits into Lake Michigan near Saugatuck. On the way it passes through two of Michigan's middle-sized manufacturing cities, Battle Creek and Kalamazoo, and many smaller towns with big histories, Homer, Albion, Marshall, Concord, Ceresco, Galesburg, Allegan, Otsego and Plainwell. A few places that were once important stops on the river, Singapore, Sheridan, Bath Mills, and Harmonia, no longer exist at all. There was a time, too, when hydroelectric dams on the Kalamazoo River furnished most of the electricity for southern Michigan.

In this volume there are chapters on the meaning of the name "Kalamazoo" and how it has been used in songs and poetry, information on the almost annual flooding and the steps taken to protect cities from the health concerns caused by water that invades homes. Environmental problems that once caused the Kalamazoo River to be known as the "sewer of West Michigan" are detailed along with some steps undertaken and to remove some of the contamination left by earlier industries.

A mile by mile trip down the river tells the history and present-day status of the settlements along its banks with many maps, old and new, and vintage postcard views.

978-1-877703-40-9 128 p, illustrated, indexed, bibliography. 2006

Rivers of Michigan Series

The Grand

The Grand River was the superhighway of early Michigan. It connected with the Saginaw River, or the Huron River, to elp travelers cross the peninsula. On its way from the Irish Hills to Grand Haven on Lake Michigan, the state's longest river passes through three major cities, Jackson, Lansing and Grand Rapids, and many smaller settlements including, Eaton Rapids, Ionia, Ada, Saranac, Eastmanville, and Lowell. A few of the old river towns have disappeared completely. Little is left to mark the former location of Kinneville, Columbia, Waverly Park, Tallmadge, Spoonville and Petrieville. Dams on the rapids at Eaton Rapids, Grand Rapids, Lansing and elsewhere furnished power for grinding wheat, turning the saws in lumbermills and manufacturing furniture. Steamboats carried a steady traffic into the 20th Century, especially on the lower river, but today the smoke-belching giants have been replaced by excursion boats taking tourists on scenic trips. Canoes, kayaks and motorized pleasure boats share the ripples.

In this volume the plans to create a cross-peninsula canal are discussed, along with the difficulties caused by floods, ice buildup, and log jams, including the famous incident in the spring of 1883 when log jams from Lowell to Grand Haven threatened every bridge along the way. Read how fishing has actually improved in the last 50 years, bringing steelhead trout as far inland as Lansing.

A mile by mile trip down the river discusses interesting history and sights along the way, where to put in and take out small boats, and is profusely illustrated with maps, old postcard views and photographs.

978-1-87773-39-3   160 p, illustrated, indexed, bibliography
2007

Rivers of Michigan Series

The Raisin

About 1780 the residents of Detroit began to look for new areas to settle. One of the first places they moved on to was a river south of the city which was Michigan Territory's only port on Lake Erie. Here the mostly French newcomers began to lay out ribbon farms on both sides of the river they called *Riviere aux Raisin*, after the wild grapes that grew in profusion along its banks. Even into the 21st Century the riverbanks pass through a mainly rural landscape, touching, also, the small cities of Tecumseh, Petersburg, and Monroe; the villages of Brooklyn, Manchester, Dundee, Blissfield, Deerfield and Clinton, and the sites of former settlements at Hamlin, Leroy, Raisin Center, Newburg and Cambridge Junction.

This volume also covers the battles on the banks of the River Raisin against the invading British and their Indian allies in 1813, floods and other disasters along the river beginning in 1836 and power creation including five of the Ford Company's "village industries," where old mill sites were put to new uses manufacturing parts for automobiles. Today the focus is on river clean-up and rehabilitation.

A mile-by-mile survey discusses interesting history and sights along the way. Years of industries and agriculture have left the river with a legacy of chemical waste which is gradually being remedied. With continuing application of government funds and local efforts the lotus plants are once more blooming on the River Raisin.

978-1-877703-04-1   112 p, illustrated, indexed, bibliography.
2009

Future projected volumes:

    The St. Joseph
    The Huron